Maura Laverty

Novelist, journalist, playwright, storyteller supreme, Maura Laverty always had an interest in cooking, a love that peeps out of almost everything she ever wrote.

Born in Rathdangan in County Kildare in 1907, she went to Spain at the age of seventeen as a governess but soon graduated to secretarial work, and began to write for a Madrid newspaper. A whirlwind romance with an Irish journalist led to marriage and three children. She continued writing and her first novel *Never No More*, published in 1942, was an immediate success. She published three more novels (all banned in Ireland until the 1960s), two children's books and her well-known cookbooks. One of her novels, dramatised as *Liffey Lane*, was produced by Hilton Edwards and Michael MacLiammoir. Another play, *Tolka Row*, became a very popular television series on RTE. She died in 1966.

Full and Plenty, her most comprehensive cookbook, was first published in 1960.

D1127228

MAURA LAVERTY

Full & Plenty

PART TWO

ANVIL BOOKS

First published in 1960 by
The Irish Flour Millers' Association

This edition published in 1985 by
Anvil Books Limited
45 Palmerston Road, Dublin 6.

2 4 6 5 3

ISBN 1 901737 30 6

Typesetting by Computertype Limited
Printed by Colour Books Limited

Contents

Useful facts and figures

Ounces don't translate into convenient metric measures. In this book they are rounded up or down to the nearest 25 grams; the table shows the exact equivalent to the nearest round figure, and the conversion used in the book.

Ounces – grams

Ounces	g equivalent	Conversion
½	14	13
1	28	25
2	57	50
3	85	75
4	113	100
5	142	150
6	170	175
7	198	200
8	227	225
9	255	250
10	283	275
11	312	300
12	340	350
13	368	375
14	397	400
15	425	425
16 (1 lb)	454	450
17	482	475
18	510	500
19	539	535
20 (1¼ lb)	567	560
24 (1½ lb)	681	675

The imperial tablespoon (Irish and English) holds approx. 17 ml. The American holds only 14 ml, and the Australian 20 ml. The teaspoon is the same in all countries.

Oven temperatures

Gas mark	F°	C°
½	250	120
1	275	140
2	300	150
3	325	165
4	350	175
5	375	190
6	400	200
7	425	220
8	450	230
9	475	240
10	500	250

The imperial (and Australian) pint is 20 fluid ounces; the American pint is 16 fluid ounces.

Liquids

Imperial	Approx. ml	Conversion
1 tbs	15	15
¼ pint	142	150
½ pint	283	275
¾ pint	426	425
1 pint	568	570
1½ pint	852	850
1¾ pint	1000	1000

Handy measures (all level tablespoons)

1 oz butter/sugar	2 tablespoons	⅛ cup
2 oz butter/sugar	4 tablespoons	¼ cup
4 oz butter/sugar	8 tablespoons	½ cup
8 oz butter/sugar	16 tablespoons	1 cup
1 oz flour	4 tablespoons	
2 oz flour	8 tablespoons	½ cup
4 oz flour	16 tablespoons	1 cup

Soup

I wish those magazine writers who lay down rules for happy marriages could have known the Dalys. Brigid was ten years older than Tom. She was an educated woman, a teacher, and the daughter of a teacher. Tom was a weedy product of the Dublin slums, who had spent four years in a reformatory. They never had a family. In spite of all this, they were the happiest married couple I have ever known.

It may have been because they possessed something which the know-all writers sometimes overlook. Brigid and Tom Daly had the thing which laughs at writers as well as at locksmiths. They had love. In addition, Brigid was a good cook.

Until she came as teacher to Dunlaney National School, few in our place had any idea of the value of herbs and garlic in cooking. But we began to take interest after hearing Brigid speak at a meeting of the Countrywoman's Association on what a tablespoonful of chives could do for an omelette, and on what a sprig of marjoram and a bay leaf could do for a stew. And when we had visited her lonely little house at Dunlaney bog and had sampled the proof of her words, we all started to spade and to clear handkerchief-sized plots for herb gardens.

The story of Tom and Brigid's meeting and courtship would make a book. She said herself that her patron saint must have had a hand in it, because it all started on St. Brigid's Day.

She had invited me out to supper. 'We'll have mutton broth,' she promised. It was a raw afternoon for the two-mile walk to Dunlaney, but I knew there would be comfort at the end of it in that mutton broth.

Brigid's mutton broth was very special. Instead of using a

sheep's head, as the rest of us did, she used lean mutton, diced small. There was eating and drinking in that broth. As you ate, it wasn't just zesty soup you spooned. Each mouthful held as well the delight of tender meat, satisfying barley and succulent vegetables. The faint incense of onion, parsley, thyme and bay leaf which hovered over the lovely brew made the name 'mutton broth' almost sacrilegious. Eaten with fingers of toast, it made a complete meal.

As I hurried up the garden path to Brigid's front door, the fragrance of my supper greeted me, making my mouth water.

I got no broth that night. When I went into the kitchen the last of it was being spooned up by a pale, undersized lad of sixteen or so, while Brigid looked on happily.

'This is Tom Daly,' she introduced.

The boy got to his feet. 'I'd better be going now,' he said awkwardly.

'Are you sure you've eaten enough?' Brigid enquired with kindness. That was the most noticeable thing about dark-haired, dark-eyed Brigid. There was kindness in every comfortable line of her.

'It was grand, thanks,' the boy stammered. 'I'm full up.'

'The bus passes below at the turn, then,' she told him. She handed him a ten-shilling note. 'Here's your fare. I know that you'll keep your word and go straight back. That you won't let me down.'

'I won't,' he promised. His heart was shining in his eyes. 'I-I won't ever forget you. Good-bye — and thanks.'

'Who was he, anyway?' I asked, when he had gone.

'He's an unfortunate lad who ran away from Murraystown Reformatory,' she told me as she busied herself clearing the table. 'I found him here when I came in from school. He broke into the house to look for something to eat. He was starved, the creature, after walking twenty miles across the bog. It was lucky I had the mutton broth ready.'

That was Brigid all over. Where another would have given the intending thief a blow, Brigid gave him a meal.

'He was full of fight at first,' she said. 'But when he saw I was sorry for him he stopped being tough, and showed himself to be only a little boy in trouble. By degrees, I got the whole story out of him — the drunken father, the stepmother who didn't want him, and money he stole to go to the pictures. Such a job as I had persuading him to go back.'

'And do you really think he'll go back?' I asked.

'I wish I was as sure of Heaven,' she said. 'I know children. Something about that boy told me he won't break his word. The poor child.'

Remembering the look he had given her as he went out the door, I could not help thinking that, whatever his age, there was more than child in Tom Daly.

She reached for the egg bowl. 'I'm afraid it will have to be an omelette after all,' she apologized. 'Do you mind?' Under the circumstances I did not mind in the least.

As he had promised, Tom Daly did not forget Brigid. When his time at Murraystown was finished, he came back to Dunlaney. Mrs. Derrigan gave him a job as a yardboy. He never looked back. From one job to another he went, bettering himself each time. When he was twenty and earning £3 a week in Logan's garage, Brigid and he started to keep company. When at twenty-five he got his good post in the briquette factory, they got married.

And it all goes to prove that though the smell of French scent may attract a man the smell of good honest broth will anchor him for ever.

Time was when the Irish housewifes' soup was merely the water in which meat was cooked. At home in Kildare, they tell a story of a certain jumped-up farmer who, one cold market-day, decided to treat himself to something better than the public house lunch of cheese sandwich and bottle of stout which was his usual fare when away from home. In the unaccustomed luxury of a restaurant he ordered a meal. The waitress noticed that his consommé remained untouched.

'Don't you like your soup, sir?' she enquired. 'You can keep it,' retorted the farmer huffily. He reached for his cap. 'Let them that ate the meat drink the soup.'

Attitudes change. Today's housewife knows that a plate of

soup is an integral part of a good meal. And she suits the soup to the quality of the dishes which follow: A clear soup to serve as an appetizer for a substantial main dish; broth, cream soup or purée to atone for calorie shortages when, for one reason or another, the main dish is light.

Soups may be divided into five classes:

1. Clear soup, sometimes known as consommé or bouillon: Clear soup depends for its attraction on zest and on clarity achieved by careful skimming and straining. For sparklingly clear consommé, clarify with the shell and white of an egg. Strain 1 quart prepared hot consommé through a linen cloth wrung out in cold water (this ensures that every particle of fat is removed). Wash an egg. Separate yolk from white. Place crushed shell and egg white in a bowl with 1 dessertspoon of cold water. Beat until frothy. Reheat the consommé but do not allow it to boil. Add egg white and shell. It will coagulate and trap all those particles which cause cloudiness. Strain the soup once more. Reheat and serve.

2. Broth, sometimes called chowder or gumbo: This is composed of stock from meat or vegetables, thickened with diced vegetables and/or meat, rice, oatmeal, barley, flour or other cereal.

3. Cream soup: Usually white stock from meat, fish or vegetables thickened with white roux (a paste of flour and fat), or with flour blended with water or kneaded with butter. The simplest cream soups are made by combining well-flavoured stock with cream sauce. For extra smoothness and richness, beaten egg is sometimes added. Bisque is another name for cream soup.

4. Purée: A good soup composed of stock from fish, vegetables or meat which are then sieved to thicken the soup.

5. Jellied Soup: Strong consommé, stiffened with aspic or reduced by quick boiling to jelly.

Soup garnishes

With clear soup: Chopped parsley or chives, thin slice of lemon or cucumber. Serve separately, grated parmesan cheese, Melba toast, tiny cheese diamonds made with cheese pastry, or cheese toast (small triangles of toast spread with grated cheese and grilled until cheese is melted).

With cream soup, broth, purée: Croutons (diced bread fried golden-brown and drained on absorbent paper — for garlic croutons, rub each slice of bread with a cut clove of garlic before frying it); batter balls (drop pancake batter by teaspoonfuls into boiling stock or soup); slice of hard cooked egg; crisp bacon crumbs; grated cheese. A spoonful of whipped cream and a sprinkling of parsley or chives adds a nice touch.

Jellied soups: Sprigs of parsley or cress, slice of lemon, sprinkling of fresh herbs, chopped olives, chives.

Note: Any soup may be made more substantial by the addition of meat balls or dumplings. Form meat balls made with hamburger recipe (page 104) into 1-inch balls. Drop into boiling soup about ten minutes before soup is done. Tiny dumplings are cooked in the same way.

Stock

Few of us nowadays have the time or space for the stockpot which used to be considered the first essential of soup-making. We use as stock the water in which meat, fish or vegetables (or trimmings from these) have been cooked. Or, failing these, we improvize stock by adding yeast extract or bouillon cubes to hot water. But it is still a good idea to buy a few marrow bones and/or 1 lb of shin beef once or twice a week and to simmer them slowly for two to three hours with a bouquet garni. Stock should be skimmed and strained, and kept in a refrigerator if not used within twenty-four hours of being made. Failing a refrigerator the stock should be reboiled to destroy any lurking bacteria. The straining of stock is important; if vegetables are left in stock it is liable to turn sour.

Use only white stock for soup that is intended to be white and creamy. The colour of meat soup or consommé may be deepened by the addition of a little browning made by cooking 1 oz sugar in a saucepan until mahogany colour (do not let it burn) and then adding $\frac{1}{2}$ pint of cold water. Bring again to a boil, strain and keep in a corked bottle. A drop or two of vegetable colour may be added to pea soup or beetroot soup.

Some helpful hints

Experienced cooks know these shortcuts to perfect soup!

A double saucepan is virtually a necessity for all those recipes which warn you not to let the mixture boil, something which is quite difficult to avoid when the saucepan is in direct contact with the heat.

To skin tomatoes — plunge them into boiling water for a few minutes. The skin then peels easily.

Too thick soup — add milk or water.

Too thin soup — several remedies here. If you have the time, take off the lid and continue simmering; this will reduce the liquid. You can also use *beurre manié* (flour and softened butter kneaded together and dropped into the soup in small balls); arrowroot is better for clear soups. If time is short, ground rice thickens quickly.

Sweating vegetables produces a good flavour. Melt the butter or margarine, add the sliced vegetables and cook, stirring or shaking well, over a low heat for 5 minutes.

Bouquet garni. This addes enormously to the flavour of practically all soups. It consists of a small sprig each of thyme, parsley, marjoram, basil, tarragon and a bay leaf, which are tied together or combined in a muslin bag. The bouquet garni is removed before erving.

Curdling. See chapter on sauces.

Roux. A roux is simply a combination of an equal amount of flour and butter blended together.

Editor's note: In Maura Laverty's day, vegetables had to be sieved to produce a smooth pureé. Now liquidizers do all the hard work.

Broths

Many doubt it, but the fact remains that every north of Ireland man has a great affinity with one of our holiest saints, St. Columba. That affinity is a love of broth. St. Columba lived on it, and there never yet was a man born north of the Boyne who could not eat it with relish every day of his life. St. Columba's favourite potage was *brothchán buidhe,* a savoury concoction of vegetable stock, thickened with oatmeal and enriched with milk. There is a story that when Lent came around the saint decided to mortify himself with ersatz broth, so he instructed the lay brother to put nothing into the broth pot except water and nettles, with a taste of salt on Sundays.

'Is nothing else to go into it, your reverence?' asked the cook in horror. 'Nothing except what comes out of the pot-stick,' the saint replied sternly.

This went on for two weeks. The saint grew thinner and weaker, and the cook grew more and more worried. And then, all of a sudden, St. Columba started to put on weight again and the worried look left the cook's face. The devoted lay brother had made himself a hollow pot-stick down which he poured milk and oatmeal. Thus he was able to preserve his master from starvation and himself from the horrible sins of disobedience and lies.

Here is the glorified version of *brothchán buidhe* which I prepared for a Saint Patrick's Day Luncheon at Cavanagh's Restaurant, New York.

Brothchán buidhe (yellow broth)	
	2 pints chicken stock (1140 ml)
	1 stalk celery
	1 medium onion
	1 small carrot
	Salt and pepper
	2 oz butter or margarine (50g)
	2 oz flour (50g)
	1 oz flake oatmeal (25g)
	4 oz chopped spinach (110g)
	2 tablespoons cream (30 ml)
	1 dessertspoon parsley

Add the chopped celery, onion and carrot to the stock, and salt and pepper to taste. Cook for 30 minutes. Knead butter and flour together and add to the stock. Sprinkle in the flakemeal, add the chopped spinach, and simmer for 15 minutes. Sieve, correct the seasoning and stir in the cream. Sprinkle with chopped parsley.

Leek broth

3 medium potatoes
2 pints stock (1140 ml)
1 lb leeks (450g)
2 oz bread (50g)
1 oz bacon fat (25g)
2 oz rice (50g)
Salt and pepper

Peel and quarter the potatoes and put into the stock. Slice the leeks and fry them, with the bread, in the fat until it has all been absorbed. Add to the stock and simmer for 30 minutes. Add the rice and simmer for another 30 minutes. Season.

Mutton broth

2 oz pearl barley (50g)
2 pints mutton stock (1140 ml)
1 medium onion
1 carrot/1 white turnip/1 leek
Heart of a small cabbage
2 oz butter or margarine (50g)
Bouquet garni
Salt and pepper

Add the barley, which has been soaked overnight, to the stock and let it simmer, covered, while you prepare the vegetables. Chop them finely, and shred the cabbage finely. Melt the butter in a frying pan and sauté the vegetables, without browning, for 3 minutes. Add them to the stock with the bouquet garni, salt and pepper, and simmer until the vegetables are tender. If a thicker broth is required, add *beurre manié* 5 minutes before the broth is cooked.

Scotch broth

3 pints cold water (1700ml)
2 lb lean mutton (900g)
4 tablespoons barley
4 tablespoons each chopped carrot, turnip, onion, celery, cabbage
2 chopped leeks
2 tablespoons butter or margarine
Salt and pepper
1 dessertspoon chopped parsley

Cut the mutton into ½-inch cubes, season and cover with the cold water. Bring quickly to boiling point, skim and add the barley, which has been soaked overnight. Simmer for 1½ hours or until the meat is tender. Fry the diced vegetables in the butter for 5 minutes. Add to the soup with salt and pepper, and continue cooking until the vegetables are tender. Finally, add the parsley.

Shin of beef may be treated this way, too, to make a very good broth known as Hough Soup. Use 3 oz of rice (75g) instead of the barley.

Vegetable broth

1 pint milk (570ml)
1 pint stock or water (570ml)
4 oz (110g) each grated carrots, turnips, potatoes, onions, parsnips
Bouquet garni
6 peppercorns (tied in muslin)
1 oz flour (50g)
1 oz butter or margarine (50g)
Salt and pepper

Combine the milk and stock in a large stewpan. Add the vegetables, bouquet garni and peppercorns. Cover and simmer for 30 minutes, then remove the bouquet garni and peppercorns. Knead the flour into the butter, add to the soup, stir well and simmer for another 5 minutes. Season.

Consommés

Chicken consommé

Bones and giblets of a chicken or boiling fowl
2–2½ pints water (1140–1400ml)
1 medium onion
4 oz carrots (110g)
2 stalks celery
Bouquet garni
2 oz vermicelli or spaghetti (50g)
Salt and pepper

Put the giblets into a large stewpan, cover with cold water, bring to the boil and simmer, covered, for 1 hour. Add the vegetables and bouquet garni, and continue simmering for another hour. Skim and strain. Place over strong heat and boil, uncovered, until reduced to 1½ pints. Sprinkle in broken vermicelli or spaghetti and simmer until cooked (10 minutes for spaghetti, 3 for vermicelli). Season.

Consommé Julienne

8 oz diced shin beef (225g)
1 lb beef bones (450g)
2 pints water (1140ml)
Salt and pepper
Browning or yeast extract
1 leek/1 carrot/1 onion
1 stalk celery
½ cup shredded lettuce
½ teaspoon sugar

Put the beef and bones into a large stewpan, cover with cold water and simmer, covered, for 1 hour. Season and add the browning or yeast extract to colour. Shred the vegetables very finely, add to the boiling stock, with the sugar, and cook for 5 minutes. A little sherry added just before serving adds the touch of perfection.

Cream soups

Cream of cauliflower

1 small cauliflower
2 pints stock or water (1140ml)
3 oz butter or margarine (75g)
3 oz flour (75g)
1 small chopped onion
Salt and pepper
1 pint milk (570ml)
2 egg yolks

Cook the cauliflower for 10 minutes in the boiling stock or water, adding salt to taste. Melt the butter, stir in the flour and cook for 2 minutes, taking care not to let it brown. Add the stock from the cauliflower, stirring well. When boiling, add the cauliflower and onion, and season. Simmer slowly for 40 minutes, then skim and sieve. Return to the heat with the milk and bring to the boil. Beat the egg yolks, adding a little of the hot mixture. Add to the soup and stir over a low heat until thick, taking care not to let it boil. Serve with cubes of fried bread.

Cream of celery

3 oz butter or margarine (75g)
1 tablespoon flour
1 pint milk (570ml)
Salt and pepper
2 head celery
1 pint stock or water (570ml)

Melt the butter, stir in the flour, and cook for 2 minutes. Add the milk to make a thin white sauce. Season. Cook the celery in stock or water until tender. Rub through a sieve and combine with the white sauce, stirring well.

Cream of cheese

2 peeled and chopped potatoes
1 large chopped onion
$1\frac{1}{2}$ pints stock (850ml)
$\frac{1}{2}$ pint milk (275ml)
4 oz grated cheese (110g)
Salt and pepper

Cook potatoes and onions, covered, in $\frac{1}{2}$ pint of stock until tender. Sieve and combine with the remaining stock and milk. Heat to boiling point, remove from the heat and stir in the grated cheese. Reheat to serving point but do not boil. Season.

Cream of chicken

1 tablespoon chopped onion
2 oz butter or margarine (50g)
2 oz flour (50g)
$1\frac{1}{2}$ pints chicken stock (850ml)
$\frac{1}{2}$ pint milk (275ml)
4 oz chopped cooked chicken (110g)
Salt and pepper
Parsley

Sauté the onion in the butter until tender. Stir in the flour and mix well. Gradually stir in the stock and milk, bring to the boil and simmer for 5 minutes. Add the chicken and season. Sprinkle with chopped parsley.

Cream of mushroom

1 tablespoon chopped onion
2 oz butter or margarine (50g)
8 oz chopped mushrooms (225g)
2 oz flour (50g)
Salt and pepper
1 pint chicken stock (570ml)
1 pint milk (570ml)

Sauté the onion in butter until tender. Add the mushrooms and cook for four minutes. Stir in the flour, and season. When bubbly, remove from the heat and gradually stir in the chicken stock and milk. Reheat to serving point.

Cream of spinach

1 dessertspoon chopped onion
2 oz butter or margarine (50g)
2 oz flour (50g)
Salt and pepper
1 pint stock (570ml)
1 pint milk (570ml)
1 lb chopped spinach (450g)

Sauté the onion in butter until tender but not coloured. Stir in the flour, salt and pepper and blend until bubbly. Cook the spinach in its own steam until tender, sieve and add to the onion mixture. Remove from the heat and add stock and milk. Reheat to serving temperature but do not boil. Serve garnished with chopped hard-cooked egg white.

Cream of tomato

2 lb chopped tomatoes (900g)
1 small chopped onion
1 pint stock or water (570ml)
Salt and pepper
A little sugar
2 oz butter or margarine (50g)
2 oz flour (50g)
1½ pints milk (850ml)

Cook the tomatoes in the stock for 15 minutes. Rub the onion and seasoning through a sieve, add a little sugar and return to the saucepan. Bring to the boil. Make a roux with the butter and flour and gradually add the milk. When smooth, stir into the tomato mixture. Reheat, season, and serve with a blob of salted whipped cream on each serving.

Cream of vegetable

3 oz butter or margarine (75g)
1 lb sliced tomatoes (450g)
1 lb sliced potatoes (450g)
1 medium chopped onion
2 pints stock (1150ml)
1 teaspoon sugar
Salt and pepper
$\frac{1}{2}$ pint milk (275ml)
1 egg yolk
4 oz cooked rice (110g)

Melt the butter, add the tomatoes, potatoes and onion and cook, stirring well, over a low heat for 5 minutes. Add the stock, sugar and seasoning, cover and simmer for 40 minutes. Sieve. Return to the heat, preferably in a double saucepan. Add the scalded milk and beaten egg yolk, taking care that the mixture does not boil and curdle. To each plateful of soup, add 2 tablespoons of the rice, which you have cooked for about 20 minutes.

Fish soup

The basis of most good fish soups is a stock made from the bones and trimmings of white fish, herbs, vegetables and seasoning. Oily fish such as mackerel and herring is not suitable.

Fish stock

$1\frac{1}{2}$ lb (675g) of fish bones and trimmings
3 sprigs parsley
1 bay leaf
2 tablespoons mushroom peelings
1 stalk celery

1 small onion/1 small carrot
4 peppercorns
Small sprig lemon thyme
2 pints of water (1140ml)

Combine the ingredients and simmer in the water for about 45 minutes. Strain through a cloth.

Cod chowder

1 lb cod (450g)
1½ cups cold water
2 rashers of bacon
4 peeled and sliced potatoes
3 tablespoons chopped onion
3 cups milk
1 oz butter or margarine (25g)
Salt and pepper

Place the fish in a saucepan with 1 cup of the water and simmer for 10 minutes. Drain the fish, reserving the liquid. Bone and skin it, then replace in the stock. Dice the bacon and fry slowly until almost all the fat is extracted. Put it into a saucepan and add the potatoes, onion, and the remaining ½ cup of water; cover and cook for 10 minutes. Add the fish and fish stock and simmer the chowder for 5 minutes. Add the milk and bring to boiling point. Just before serving, add the butter, then salt and pepper to taste.

This chowder may be made in advance and reheated, but it must not be allowed to boil.

Cod soup

1 cod's head
2 stalks chopped celery
2 small onions stuck with cloves
1 chopped carrot
1 small chopped white turnip
2 pints fish stock (1140ml)
2 oz butter or margarine (50g)
2 oz flour (50g)
1 pint milk (570ml)
Salt and pepper

Simmer the cod's head and vegetables in the stock for 45 minutes. Strain. Make a roux with the butter and flour, and add the milk to make a cream sauce. Add the liquor from the cod's head, reheat to serving point, season and serve with chopped chives.

Fish cream soup

3 chopped leeks
1 stalk chopped celery
2 oz butter (50g)
2 oz flour (50g)
1½ pints fish stock (850ml)
Salt and pepper
1 beaten egg
2 tablespoons cream (30ml)

Sauté the leeks and celery in the butter for 5 minutes. Sprinkle in the flour, stir well and gradually add the stock, salt and pepper. Simmer for 15 to 20 minutes. Add the beaten egg to a little of the hot soup, return to the saucepan and cook for another 2 minutes, without boiling. Stir in the cream and serve garnished with shrimps.

Mussel soup

3 pints mussels
1 chopped onion
1 sprig parsley
1 glass cider
2 oz butter (50g)
2 oz flour (50g)
2 chopped leeks
1 chopped stalk celery
2 pints scalded milk (1140ml)
Salt and pepper
¼ teaspoon grated nutmeg
2 tablespoons cream (30ml)

Place the washed mussels in a saucepan, with the onion, parsley and cider. Cover and place over moderate heat, shaking the saucepan frequently. Remove from heat as soon as the mussels open. Strain through a fine cloth, reserving the liquid. Sauté the leeks and celery in the butter (without browning), sprinkle in the flour and stir well. Add the scalded milk, seasoning and nutmeg, and simmer for 20 minutes. Put through a sieve, add the liquor from the mussels, the cream and the mussels. Reheat to serving point.

Purées

Carrot purée

1 lb thinly sliced carrot (450g)
1 pint stock or water (570ml)
8 oz sliced tomatoes (225g)
1½ oz butter or margarine (38g)
1 pint milk (570ml)
Salt and pepper

Cook the carrots in stock or water until tender. Drain and mash, reserving the water. Sauté the tomatoes in butter, without allowing them to brown, until all the fat is absorbed. Bring the milk to the boil, add the carrot water, carrots, tomatoes, and season. Simmer for 20 minutes.

Haricot bean soup

8 oz haricot beans (225g)
8 oz sliced tomatoes (225g)
1 large chopped onion
2 oz butter or margarine (50g)
2½ pints stock (1400ml)
Salt and pepper

Wash the beans, cover with cold water and soak overnight (unless you are using the quick-cooking variety).   Sauté the tomatoes and onion in butter for about 5 minutes. Add the strained beans and the stock, and simmer gently until they are tender. Season, rub through a sieve, reheat and serve very hot, with croutons.

Kidney soup

12 oz thinly sliced beef kidney (350g)
8 oz lean chopped beef (225g)
1 chopped onion
1 chopped turnip
1 chopped carrot
3 sticks chopped celery

2 tablespoons flour
Salt and pepper
2 oz butter or margarine (50g)
2 pints stock or water (1140ml)

Coat the kidney, beef and vegetables in the seasoned flour and sauté in the butter until it is all absorbed. Add the stock or water, cover and simmer until tender. Rub through a sieve, keeping back some of the kidney to chop and use as a garnish. Reheat before serving.

Lentil soup

6 oz lentils (175g)
2 pints stock (1140ml)
Salt and pepper
1 large chopped onion
1 oz butter or margarine (25g)
1 dessertspoon flour
$\frac{1}{2}$ pint hot milk (275ml)

Wash and soak the lentils overnight (unless they are the quick-cooking variety). Drain and put into a saucepan with the stock, salt and pepper. Add the onion and bring to the boil. Simmer, skimming occasionally, until the lentils are soft. Rub through a sieve and return to the saucepan. Knead the butter with the flour, add to the soup and stir until it has boiled. Add the hot milk, garnish with parsley and serve.

Pea soup

1 lb peas (450g)
2 oz lean ham (50g) or 1 ham bone
1 medium onion and clove
$\frac{1}{2}$ head diced celery
1 chopped carrot
2 pints stock (1140ml)
$\frac{1}{2}$ pint hot milk (275ml)
Salt and pepper
Mint

Put the peas into a saucepan with the diced ham or ham bone, the onion with the clove stuck into it, the celery, carrot and stock. Bring to the boil and simmer until the peas are soft. Remove the onion and bone and rub the soup through a sieve.

Return to the saucepan, and add the hot milk and seasoning.
Serve very hot with finely chopped mint.

Potato soup

8 medium peeled and diced potatoes
Water
2 medium chopped onions
2 tablespoons butter or margarine
Salt and pepper
$\frac{1}{8}$ teaspoon nutmeg
1 egg
$\frac{1}{2}$ pint milk (275ml)

Cook the potatoes until tender, then drain and reserve 3 cups
of the water. Put the potatoes through a sieve. Sauté the onions
in butter until slightly browned. Into the potato water, put the
potatoes and onion. Season, then add the slightly beaten egg,
milk and nutmeg. Heat, but do not boil, stirring constantly.

Tinned bean soup

1 medium tin beans in tomato sauce
1 large chopped onion
2 large chopped potatoes
2 pints stock (1140ml)
Salt and pepper
1 oz butter (25g)

Put the beans, onions and potatoes into the stock, season and
simmer until tender. Rub through a sieve, reheat and stir in
the butter before serving.

Tomato soup (jellied)

1 lb tomatoes (450g)
8 oz chopped carrots (225g)
4 oz chopped leeks (110g)
1 medium chopped onion
2 pints stock (1140ml)
1 oz gelatine (25g)
Salt and pepper

Put the vegetables into the stock and simmer for about an
hour. Soften the gelatine for 5 minutes in 2 tablespoons of cold
water. Add 1 cup of the hot soup and stir until the gelatine is
dissolved. Add the remaining soup, season, pour into bouillon
cups and leave until set.

Fish

For the proof of what a good fish dinner can do for romance there is no need to look further than Barney Malone.

Barney was a sore thorn in the side of our Fishery Board. From February to August, not a salmon in the river was safe from him. The Board had never been able to pin anything on Barney. But in a small place like ours no lawbreaker can hide his misdeeds.

Barney could not have been called a poacher in the ordinary sense. Never in a million years would he have descended to the depravity of using a net. And as for killing a female salmon during the spawning season — well, that was an iniquity no one could have laid at Barney's door. He was a decent and a likeable lad. But, there it was; he was the victim of some mysterious compulsion which impelled him irresistibly towards salmon.

Barney might be walking along the river bank dressed in his best on a Sunday evening. He might be thinking of the wrongs of Ireland, or the red hair of Nellie Ryan, or the way Nellie's father opposed the match because Barney would not stay in a steady job. He might be musing on anything under the sun except fish. But the minute he would hear a splash or see a silver gleam, into the water with him, Sunday clothes and all. Out with his gaff, then, and in the next to no time the river would be one salmon less, and Barney's craving would have found temporary appeasement.

'It's a mania with him,' Mr. Hennessy of the Fishery Board often said. 'The river draws him the way the public house draws other men. But a stop will have to be put to his gallop.

The first time we catch him, he'll go to jail.'

The question was: Who was going to catch him?

That was the problem bothering Mr. Hennessy as he walked along the road one evening. Old Sam Wheeler, who had been water-bailiff for forty years, was due to be retired. If only we could get the right kind of man to replace him, Mr. Hennessy mused wistfully. The right kind of active energetic man, a man who'd catch Malone with a salmon.

He came to the cottage where Barney's girl lived with her father, the Thatcher Ryan. He stopped and looked at the neat little house with its whitewashed walls and shining new thatch.

Isn't Malone the young fool? he marvelled. There's that grand little girl, and she's mad about him. There's a lovely home waiting for him to hang up his hat in, if only he'd give up the poaching and get himself a steady job. There's no doubt he needs a spell in jail. It would teach him a lesson.

All of a sudden, Mr. Hennessy's nostrils twitched. Through the open window of the cottage was wafted a delicious smell of salmon frying in butter.

Mr. Hennessy crept nearer the window. On a pan on the fire, two thick and rosy salmon steaks sizzled tunefully. The poacher himself was there, sitting comfortably back in his chair. With as carefree an air as if the salmon had been caught legally, Barney looked on while his girl cooked the fish.

Mr. Hennessy threw open the door and walked in. 'Caught at last, Malone!' he said. A legacy of ten thousand pounds would not have given him greater glee. 'It's the jail for you, my lad.'

Barney took it gamely. 'Fair enough, Mr. Hennessy.' He threw one leg over the other, and his face took on a happily reminiscent look. 'Anyway,' he said, 'I had a good run for my money.'

Nellie was not equipped with her lover's fortitude. She burst into tears. Through her sobs, she let Mr. Hennessy know that this meant the end of her romance, that her father had sworn that Barney would never put a wedding-ring on her finger if the boy ever saw the inside of a jail. She wept and entreated and begged. And the more she wept, the greater grew Mr. Hennessy's embarrassment.

Even the chairman of a Fishery Board may have a flesh-and-blood heart. Even a stern official may have sufficient ordinary humanity to sympathize with the distractions of a young and pretty girl who is in love and who sees her loved one in danger of being whipped away from her. Mr. Hennessy was in a difficult position. There he was with the responsibility on him of ruining the happiness of two young people. At the same time, he was a conscientious and a serious-minded man. He had to remember his duty to the Board. 'I see no way out of it,' he said gruffly. 'The whole country knows that Malone has been asking for jail ever since he was old enough to handle a gaff.'

Nellie stifled her sobs and dried her eyes. 'Since you're here and since it's ready, wouldn't you have a bite to eat, Mr. Hennessy?' Her voice was small and forlorn. 'My share of the supper will be thrown out if you don't take it, for I'm that upset this minute I couldn't touch it for all the gold in Ireland.'

The suggestion made Mr. Hennessy rear back in horror. How could she imagine that he, the chairman of the Fishery Board, would share such a repast? 'Have sense, girl,' he grunted, reaching with the tongs for a coal to light his pipe.

For some reason, his pipe refused to draw for him and he had to put it back in his pocket. Maybe the way his mouth was watering was to blame. No living man could have savoured tobacco while watching Nellie Ryan dish up that meal.

Looking pathetically sad and subdued, she slithered the browned and buttery steaks on to hot plates. To the north and south of each steak she spooned little onions and baby carrots that had simmered in cream. At the east and west she placed mealy boiled potatoes. 'Let it be wasted if it must,' she lamented resignedly, as she put the steaming plates on the table and filled two blue-ringed mugs with fresh buttermilk. 'I'm that demented this minute, I'd choke if I tried to swallow the smallest little mouthful.' She sighed in a way that wrung Mr. Hennessy's heart. 'I'll leave you now while I try to work some of the desperation out of myself by getting in the fowl for the night.'

Barney Malone felt no qualms about doing justice to that supper. He pulled his chair to the table. 'Even a murderer,' said he, 'is allowed a good feed before he goes to the gallows. Since you're sending me to jail, this will likely be the last decent feed I'll be getting for a while.'

He set to. Mr. Hennessy averted his eyes. He began to be very conscious of the fact that he had not eaten since mid-day.

'There's no doubt that Nellie is a prize cook,' Barney commented. 'This bit of salmon is done to a turn. And I always say that nothing goes so well with salmon as young vegetables done in cream the way Nellie cooks them.'

Mr. Hennessy swallowed. 'It *does* seem a pity to throw out that second plateful,' he said weakly. 'When you think of the starving people in India, it seems a mortal sin to waste anything in the line of food.'

'A deadly sin,' Barney agreed. 'Sit in to the table, man, while it's still fit to eat.'

Mr. Hennessy sat in. For ten blissful minutes, there was no sound save the satisfying symphony of cutlery and delph.

When Mr. Hennessy finally pushed away his empty plate, he knew that warm glow of benevolence which always results from a satisfactory gastronomic experience.

'You're the world's biggest fool, Malone,' said he, 'not to take a steady job and settle down with that little girl. Nowhere in the world will you find her equal as a cook.'

'Nor would I find a girl to match Nellie in any other respect,' Barney agreed. 'But not even for Nellie would I make myself a prisoner in a factory or a shop. And if I did, I'd be doing her a wrong, for I'd end up by driving her as mad as the job would drive me.'

It was then that inspiration came to Mr. Hennessy. 'I wonder,' he said, 'would there be any truth in the saying that you've to set a thief to catch a thief? How would you like to be water-bailiff when Sam Wheeler retires next month?'

'It's the only steady job in the world that I'd want to take,' Barney answered.

'But mind you, if I recommend you, you musn't let me down,' Mr. Hennessy warned him. 'There must be no more poaching.'

'I'll see to that, Mr. Hennessy,' said Nellie from the doorway, and there was a light in her eye which told both men that Barney's poaching days were ended.

Being the good cook she was, I am sure that Nellie would have achieved just as satisfactory results with a couple of herrings. Because at the knee of her Aunt Mary, who for thirty years had been cook to a retired English colonel whose God was his stomach, Nellie had learned the Nine Commandments of fish cooking.

For once, I am with the Government. It *is* lamentable that we who live in an island should neglect the good food which abounds around our shores, and the equally valuable food which attracts anglers from all over the world to our river banks.

What has happened to us that we have lost our interest in fish? That this interest once was strong is proved by the repeated references to fish in our ancient literature. Remember the Salmon of Knowledge? Wasn't it with a fish dish that Saint Brigid taught a badly needed lesson to a greedy young nun? When Findabhair, daughter of the King of Connaught, wished to impress a visiting prince, it was with a fish dish that she charmed him. And once, when Saint Mochna was in the depths of despair, an unexpected gift of fish restored the man's faith in Providence.

The monks of days gone by knew that well-fed means well-read and well-adjusted. And to make sure of a plentiful supply of good food, each monastery had its well-stocked fish-pond. Maybe they lacked our knowledge of the exact dietary qualities of fish, but they had demonstrable proof of the benefits of fish-eating in their untroubled digestion, and in the limitless energy which enabled them to work half the night on their manuscripts after a heavy day of harvesting crops and souls.

In Norway and Scotland, fish is held to be a more valuable

food than meat. Whether these hardy people are mistaken or not, there is no doubt that fish is a good source of the protein needed for body-building and repairs. All fish contains the gelatine which, when combined with other foods, makes a valuable contribution to health. And the iodine contained in sea fish is an essential of correct diet.

Fish, except the more expensive kinds, calls for care and thought in the cooking. It presents a challenge to the woman who would like to give her family attractive meals at moderate cost. These recipes may help you to meet this challenge successfully.

The commandments governing good fish cooking may be reduced to these:

1. Buy only fish with clear gills, full bright eyes, firm flesh and fresh agreeable odour.

2. When boiling fish, use barely enough water to cover. When practicable, fish should be steamed. Take a tip from the French, and preserve the fish juices by wrapping fish to be boiled in a strait-jacket of buttered paper or aluminium foil.

3. Add flavour to insipid fish by adding a bouquet garni and plenty of seasoning to the cooking water. A little wine or cider added to the water helps. And this flavoured stock should be used to make fish soup or sauce.

4. Do not overcook. Fish is ready when the flesh comes easily from the bone; or, if filletted, when a creamy substance begins to run from the fish.

5. Baste generously when grilling fish. Small whole fish should be gashed to allow heat to penetrate and fat to lubricate.

6. Fish fried in shallow fat gains in appearance and flavour by being given a crisp coating of egg-and-breadcrumbs. Dip the prepared fish first in seasoned flour (with or without a sprinkling of dried herbs), then in beaten egg, and then in fine breadcrumbs.

7. When frying cutlets, fillets or whole small fish in deep fat, follow the rules for batter frying given in the section on left-overs.

8. Baked fish, whether whole or in cutlets or fillets, gains in

savour from an appetizing stuffing. Form extra stuffing into small balls, and poach in stock or toast in the baking pan, and serve with the fish.

9. Serve a discreetly seasoned and carefully flavoured sauce, suiting the sauce to the fish. Sauce is to food what an accompanist is to a singer — it should complement and enhance but it must never steal the limelight.

To prepare fish

Cleaning fish: Slit the fish at the stomach (the position varies according to the fish), remove the entrails and wash with salted water. Scrape away the black membrane which would give the cooked fish a bitter taste.

Filletting fish: For flat fish, first cut off the fins. Then with a sharp knife, cut along each side of the backbone. Slide the knife along between bones and flesh, drawing away the fillet with the left hand as you work. Remove the left-hand fillet by working towards the head; then turn the fish and, with the head towards you, remove the right-hand fillet, working towards the tail.

Herrings, mackerel, and other round fish should be cut right through the back as far as the bone; then fillet as for flat fish.

Scaling fish: Hold fish by the tail. Using a blunt knife, scrape from the tail to the head in quick firm strokes.

Basic cooking methods

Baked fish: Place prepared fish in a well-greased casserole. Sprinkle with salt, pepper and lemon juice, and dot with butter or margarine. Cover and bake for 10 to 15 minutes per lb according to the thickness of the fish (375°-gas mark 5).

Baked fish (in milk): Melt 2 tablespoons of butter in a baking tin. Put the fish into the tin and sprinkle with seasoning (salt and pepper, ⅛ teaspoon nutmeg, a bay leaf and 2 peppercorns). Add ½ pint (275ml) of scalded milk, cover and bake for about 20 minutes at 375° (gas mark 5).

The liquid in which the fish was baked can be used to make egg, parsley or anchovy sauce.

Batter-coated fish: Heat the fat in fish fryer to 375° (gas mark 5), until a cube of bread will brown in 50 seconds . Dip fish in seasoned flour, then in batter. Let excess batter drip off, lower the fish into the boiling fat and fry until golden-brown (4 to 7 minutes). Drain on kitchen paper and serve with lemon slices and tartare sauce.

Boiled fish: Rub prepared white fish with cut lemon to keep the flesh white. Wrap in buttered paper or in aluminium foil. Place in simmering salted water containing a bouquet garni, a few peppercorns and a little vinegar. Cover closely and cook gently — the length of time will depend on the thickness of the fish (a rough guide is 8 to 10 minutes per lb). Avoid overcooking. Serve on a hot plate with egg, parsley, or mousseline sauce.

Fried fish (1): Sprinkle small fish, cutlets or fillets with salt. Dip in buttermilk, then in seasoned flour. Heat butter in a frying-pan and fry the fish until golden-brown on each side, allowing about 5 minutes to each side. Serve sprinkled with chopped parsley and garnished with lemon slices.

Fried fish (2): Wipe the prepared fish. Dip in seasoned flour, then in egg beaten with a tablespoon of water, and finally in fine breadcrumbs. Gently shake off loose crumbs and fry until golden-brown in shallow or deep fat.

Grilled fish: Brush prepared fish with melted butter or oil, dust lightly with flour and season with salt and pepper. Whole fish should be gashed to allow the heat to penetrate. Pre-heat the grill at full heat, then reduce to moderate, and grill fish on greased gridiron until cooked. Turn once or more depending on thickness of fish. Serve with *maitre d'hôtel* butter, or with mustard or tartare sauce.

Steamed fish: Sprinkle prepared fish with salt and lemon juice. Place in a greased steamer or on a rack over a few inches of boiling water. Cover closely and cook over constantly boiling water until done. Steamed fish will take from 15 to 25 minutes per lb, depending on thickness. Serve with Hollandaise sauce.

Small cutlets or fillets may be steamed between two plates over boiling water.

Bass

If big, cut into steaks and boil, grill or bake like salmon. If small, grill, fry or bake like mullet. Serve with Hollandaise sauce.

Brill

Brill (scalloped)

1 lb cooked brill (450g)
3 tablespoons boiled rice
1½ tablespoons chutney
1 teaspoon grated onion
2 tablespoons sieved stewed apple
Salt and pepper
2 tablespoons fine breadcrumbs
2 oz butter (50g)

Flake the fish and combine with the rice, chutney, onion, and apple. Season and place the mixture in a greased casserole, top with the crumbs, dot with the butter and bake for 10 minutes at 375° (gas mark 5).

Cockles

Cockles (scalloped)

4 pints cockles (1 pint per person)
1 glass cider or white wine
4 oz fine breadcrumbs (110g)
2 oz butter or margarine (50g)
Salt and pepper

Wash the cockles well and leave for 1 hour in slightly salted water. Drain, place in a pan, and add the cider or white wine. Cover closely and cook for about 5 minutes over moderate heat (shaking the pan frequently) until the shells open. Remove the cockles from the shells and reserve the liquor.

Place a layer of seasoned breadcrumbs on a large fireproof dish or in individual dishes, and pile the cockles on top. Cover with breadcrumbs, moisten with the cockle liquor, dot with butter and bake for 10 minutes at 450° (gas mark 8).

Cod

Cod (creamed)

2 lb cod cutlets or fillets (900g)
½ pint cheese sauce (275ml)
2 tablespoons breadcrumbs
2 tablespoons grated cheese
2 tablespoons butter

Steam cod as directed for steamed fish. Place in a hot shallow fireproof dish. Cover with the sauce, sprinkle with the breadcrumbs and grated cheese, dot with butter and place under grill or in a hot oven until the topping browns.

Cod (salt, Biscay-style)

1 lb salt cod (450g)
2 small chopped onions
1 chopped leek
2 tablespoons butter or oil
½ clove minced garlic
1 bay leaf
Pinch of saffron
¾ pint water (425ml)
8 oz skinned and sliced tomatoes (225g)
6 quartered potatoes
1 glass sherry
Pepper

Cut the cod into 2-inch squares and soak overnight in cold water. Drain and parboil in clear water, then drain and pick out the bones. Sauté the onions and leeks in butter, then add the garlic, bay leaf, saffron blended with the water, tomatoes, potatoes, sherry and cod. Season with pepper. Bring to the boil and simmer gently until the potatoes are tender. Before serving, remove the bay leaf.

Cod (stuffed)

2 lb cod cutlets or fillets (900g)
    or 1 small codling
8 oz poultry stuffing (225)
4 oz rashers (110g)
2 oz butter or margarine (50g)

Sprinkle fish with salt, and rub the inside with a cut lemon. If whole, stuff loosely with the stuffing and stitch it up; if using fillets or cutlets, spread half with the stuffing, lay the rest on top, and tie or skewer. Place on a rack in a shallow tin, and put strips of bacon on top. Baste frequently with melted butter. Bake at 400° (gas mark 6) for about 35 minutes.

Crab

Crab (boiled)
Choose medium-sized crabs with large claws. Plunge them into boiling salted water (1 dessertspoon of salt to 1 quart of water). The crabs should be well covered with water. Boil quickly for about 20 minutes until red. Drain and let cool.

To serve: Break off claws and legs from cooked crab and remove the meat. Remove the part just under the head (this is called 'the apron'). Force the shell apart and discard the spongy material. Serve the crab meat as a salad with mayonnaise; or heat in a good cream sauce and use as an omlette filling.

Crab (dressed)
Cook as for boiled crab, then mix the body meat with French dressing. Wash and dry the shell and brighten by rubbing with oil. Fill with the dressed crab meat and serve garnished with meat from the claws and legs.

Crayfish
This miniature lobster is cooked like crab, allowing only 1 teaspoon of salt to a quart of boiling water.

Dabs
These flat fish are cousins of the plaice but much more delicate. If small, fry whole (see fried fish) and serve garnished with parsley and lemon slices. If large, fillet them, remove the skin, and coat with egg and breadcrumbs; fry until golden-brown in deep or shallow fat and serve with tartare sauce.

Haddock *(dried or Finnan)*

Poach haddock gently in a mixture of milk and water for about 10 to 15 minutes, according to thickness. Serve with a little of the liquid in which it was cooked, with a nut of butter added.

A popular way of serving is with an egg poached in the fish liquor.

Haddock (fried)

1 tablespoon flour
1 dessertspoon chopped parsley
½ teaspoon dried herbs
Salt and pepper
1½ lb filletted haddock (675g)
1 beaten egg
4 tablespoons fine breadcrumbs

Mix the flour with the parsley, herbs and seasoning. Cut the fillets into long strips about 1 inch wide, dip them in the flour, then in the egg and breadcrumbs. Tie each fillet in a small knot and fry until golden-brown. Serve around a mould of mashed potatoes. Garnish with parsley sprigs and lemon slices, and serve tomato purée separately.

Haddock (savoury)

1 lb boiled or steamed haddock (450g)
Salt and pepper
2 beaten eggs
¾ pint thin cream sauce (425ml)
4 tablespoons fine breadcrumbs
1 tablespoon butter
1 dessertspoon chopped parsley

Remove the skin and bones from the haddock. Flake the fish and place in a greased casserole. Season. Add the egg to the cream sauce and pour over the fish. Cover with crumbs, sprinkle with parsley and dot with butter. Bake for 25 minutes at 350° (gas mark 5).

Haddock on toast

Cut into rectangles, grill for a few minutes and serve on buttered toast. Streaky rashers can be wrapped around the fish.

Hake

Hake (baked)

4 cutlets hake
Salt and pepper
1 teaspoon lemon juice
Bouquet garni
¼ pint stock (150ml)
¼ pint milk (150ml)
2 tablespoons breadcrumbs
1 oz butter (25g)

Place the fish in a baking dish, and add the seasoning, lemon juice, bouquet garni, stock and milk. Sprinkle with the breadcrumbs, dot with butter, and bake for 40 minutes at 350° (gas mark 5). Serve with a little of the strained liquor.

Herrings

Herring is one of the most nutritious of all fish.

With mustard sauce
Wash, scale and clean the herrings. Place in a greased dish, cover with greased paper and bake for 25 to 30 minutes at 350° (gas mark 5). Serve with mustard sauce.

Kippered herrings
Place in a deep frying-pan, cover with hot water and bring to the boil. Cook for 1 minute, then drain and serve with a piece of butter on each kipper.

Kippers may also be grilled or fried. Brush with melted butter or margarine, sprinkle with flour and grill or fry for about 3 minutes to each side.

Bloaters are cooked in the same way as kippers.

Soused herrings
Clean and dry the herrings. Cut off heads, tails and fins, split the fish from head to tail and remove the backbones. Season, roll up and place in a pie dish. Cover with a liquid made of ¼ pint of water (150ml) and ¼ pint of vinegar (150ml), seasoned with a blade of mace, a bay leaf, 4 cloves and 3 peppercorns. Cover and bake for 50 minutes at 350° (gas mark 5).

Lobster

Boiled lobster

Cook as for crab, allowing 12 minutes to the lb. Drain and cool. Remove the claws. With a sharp knife, split the lobster open from head to tail and right through the tail. Remove the black vein, the small sac at the back of the head and the spongy material. Crack the claws gently with a hammer, taking care not to splinter them. Serve hot with melted butter, or cold with salad and mayonnaise.

Boiled, French style

Lightly brown in 2 teaspoons of olive oil, a small onion, a small carrot and a stick of celery, all sliced thinly. Add 2 tablespoons of dry sherry, $2\frac{1}{2}$ cups of water, 1 tablespoon tarragon vinegar, 4 peppercorns and a bay leaf. Salt lightly and bring to the boil. Add the lobster, cover and simmer for 12 to 15 minutes or until the lobster is very red. Remove and cool. Take the meat from the shell, coat with mayonnaise and serve with salad.

Broiled lobster

Boil lobster for 5 minutes. Split open as for boiled lobster and with a sharp knife make 2 cross cuts in the tail to prevent curling. Brush with melted butter and cook for 5 minutes under a moderate grill. Turn, brush with butter and grill the other side for 5 minutes. Serve with melted butter and lemon slices.

Lobster Newburg

Cut the meat from a boiled lobster into chunks. Place in a well-buttered saucepan, add 1 tablespoon of Madeira and sauté until practically dry. Add $\frac{1}{2}$ pint of cream and fish stock, and thicken with *beurre manié*. Serve with rice.

Stuffed lobster

Make stuffing with chopped red roe and green liver sautéed in butter. Add 2 tablespoons of breadcrumbs $\frac{1}{2}$ teaspoon chopped onion, $\frac{1}{2}$ teaspoon parsley and $\frac{1}{4}$ teaspoon thyme. Season to taste. Boil and clean the lobster and stuff the cavity with the prepared forcemeat. Bake for 12 to 15 minutes at 450° (gas mark 8).

Mackerel

Mackerel (savoury)

4 small mackerel
1 oz flour (25g)
Salt and pepper
½ teaspoon dried herbs
1 oz butter or margarine (25g)
1 teaspoon vinegar
¼ teaspoon dry mustard
½ teaspoon anchovy essence
2 tablespoons cider (30ml)

Wash and clean the mackerel, split from head to tail and remove the backbone. Dry and dip in the flour mixed with salt, pepper and dried herbs. Fry in hot fat over moderate heat, allowing 6 minutes to each side. Melt the butter in a small saucepan, add the vinegar, mustard, anchovy essence and cider. Bring to the boil and pour over the mackerel.

Because mackerel is an oily fish, a fruit sauce (made from gooseberries or rhubarb) makes an excellent accompaniment.

Mackerel (soused)

Wash and clean the mackerel. Cut off the heads and fins, split open and remove the backbones and tails. Roll up and place in a deep pie dish. Add 1 pint of wine vinegar (570ml), a bay leaf, 1 teaspoon of salt, 6 peppercorns, 3 sprigs of parsley, 1-inch stick of cinnamon and a few grains of cayenne. Cover and simmer for 45 minutes at 350° (gas mark 5).

Mullet

Grey mullet

Cook like cod, hake or whiting.

Red mullet

This is very delicate fish and is never drawn; pull out the gills but leave the trail. To preserve the delicate flavour, cook it *en papillotte* — wrapped in greased paper or aluminium foil. Sprinkle the prepared fish with seasoned flour, wrap in generously buttered paper or foil, placed in a greased dish and bake for 25–30 minutes at 350° (gas mark 5). Carefully unwrap the cooked fish, place on a hot dish and pour the liquor over it.

Mussels

Mussels are prepared and cooked like cockles.

Oysters

It seems a pity to do anything with oysters but serve them in their natural goodness, with lemon and brown bread and butter. However, they are delicious dipped in seasoned flour, then in egg and breadcrumbs and fried golden-brown in deep fat. Drain on absorbent paper and serve with cut lemon and hot tartare sauce.

Oysters Florentine

Poach the oysters in their own liquor, drain, and remove beards. Place a tablespoon of buttered cooked spinach in scallop shells, put a few oysters on top, and cover with cheese sauce. Sprinkle with grated cheese and brown for about 5 minutes at 400° (gas mark 6).

Oyster savoury (angels on horseback)

Wrap raw oysters in thin rashers of streaky bacon. Place the rolls on skewers (5 or 6 to a skewer) and grill for about 6 minutes, turning the skewers frequently. Arrange on toast and sprinkle with fried seasoned breadcrumbs.

Oyster stew

Poach oysters in stock, drain, and remove beards. Reduce stock by quick boiling, and add an equal amount of milk or cream, thickened slightly with butter and flour. Simmer for 3 minutes and season. Add the oysters and reheat but do not boil.

Pike

This fish is beloved by the French who use it a lot, especially for stuffings; it is a fish we Irish still have to develop a taste for! Pike may be boiled or steamed but it is best baked. Choose a small pike for flavour and tenderness, and when cleaning the fish remove and discard the roe.

Pike (stuffed and baked)

1 pike (about 3 lbs)
Salt and pepper
1 cup poultry stuffing
4 oz streaky rashers (110g)
1 glass sherry or cider
2 oz butter (50g)

Clean, trim and scale the fish. Wipe well, season the cavity with salt and pepper and fill loosely with the stuffing. Sew up, and place in a greased baking tin. Cover with the bacon and bake for 50 minutes at 375° (gas mark 5), basting frequently with the sherry and melted butter. Serve with tartare sauce.

Plaice

Plaice (fried)

1½ lb fillets of plaice (675g)
1 tablespoon flour
Salt and pepper
½ teaspoon grated lemon rind

Wipe the fillets and dip in flour mixed with salt, pepper and lemon rind. Fry in hot fat over moderate heat. Serve with mushroom sauce, or garnished with lemon slices and parsley.

Plaice (grilled)

4 medium sized plaice
2 tablespoons lemon juice (30ml)
Salt and pepper
1½ tablespoons olive oil (25ml)

Clean and wash fish, removing black skin. Sprinkle each side with lemon juice and seasoning, and leave for 20 minutes. Brush with oil and grill for 5 to 8 minutes on each side, according to thickness. Serve with lemon, parsley and *maître d'hôtel* butter.

Prawns

These are usually sold ready boiled. Shelled and served with mayonnaise, they make an excellent hors d'oeuvre or salad.

Or they can be sautéed in butter, flamed in brandy and served in a cream and wine sauce thickened with *beurre manié*.

Fried prawns
Shell the prawns, dip in egg and breadcrumbs and fry golden-brown in hot fat. Drain, garnish with parsley and serve with tartare sauce.

Prawn cocktail
Shred a head of lettuce and put into small dishes. Divide cooked prawns among the dishes. Cover with mayonnaise blended with 1 tablespoon of beet juice and a few drops of tabasco sauce. Garnish with chopped parsley.

Salmon

Baked salmon

4 salmon steaks
1 tablespoon olive oil (15ml)
1 tablespoon lemon juice (15ml)
1 oz butter (25g)
1 oz flour (25g)
½ pint scalded milk (275ml)
1 cup cooked and puréed spinach
1 teaspoon chopped parsley
Salt and pepper
1 beaten egg yolk
1 tablespoon cream (15ml)

Brush the salmon steaks with olive oil and lemon juice. Bake for 20 minutes at 375° (gas mark 5). Melt the butter, blend in the flour, and add the scalded milk. Simmer for 3 minutes, stirring well. Stir in the spinach purée and the seasonings, bring again to the boil and simmer for 5 minutes. Remove from the heat and add a little of the mixture to the beaten egg. Return to the sauce, add the cream and cook, without boiling, for 2 minutes. Pour over the cooked salmon and garnish with lemon wedges sprinkled with parsley.

Boiled salmon
Scale and clean the fish, washing well. Wrap in buttered paper or aluminium foil and place in boiling salted water. Bring to

the boil and skim. Cover and simmer until cooked. For a thick cut allow 10 minutes to the lb. Drain and serve with Hollandaise sauce. Garnish with sliced cucumber.

Tinned salmon
The following receipes are for tinned salmon, but can be used for any cooked fish.

Salmon cakes with mushroom sauce	**1 cup tinned salmon** **½ cup crushed cream crackers** **2 beaten eggs** **Salt and pepper** **2 tablespoons butter or margarine (30ml)** **4 oz mushrooms (110g)** **1 pint medium white sauce (570ml)** **1 tablespoon chopped chives**

Flake and bone the salmon. Mix with the cracker crumbs, eggs and seasoning. Form into patties and brown on both sides in some of the butter. Sauté the mushrooms in the rest of the butter for about 5 minutes. Add the mushrooms to the sauce, with the chives. Garnish with parsley.

Salmon croquettes	**½ pint thick cream sauce (275ml)** **1½ cups drained and flaked salmon** **2 cups mashed potatoes** **1½ teaspoons anchovy paste** **Pepper** **2 beaten eggs** **1 teaspoon lemon juice** **1 breakfastcup fine breadcrumbs** **1 tablespoon minced parsley**

Combine all the ingredients except 1 egg, the breadcrumbs and parsley. Shape into croquettes, dip in beaten egg and breadcrumbs and fry until golden-brown in hot fat. Drain and serve garnished with parsley.

Salmon loaf

1 cup flaked and boned salmon
1½ breakfastcups breadcrumbs
2 hard-boiled eggs
1 breakfastcup thick white sauce

Mix the salmon with the breadcrumbs, chopped eggs and white sauce. Place in a buttered casserole and bake for 35 minutes at 375° (gas mark 5). Serve with a piquant sauce made by adding a chopped hard-boiled egg and 2 tablespoons of chopped pickles to ½ pint (275ml) of medium white sauce.

Salmon puffs

1 tin salmon
1 beaten egg
1 teacup breadcrumbs
1 tablespoon lemon juice (15ml)
2 tablespoons grated onion
1 tablespoon melted butter
Salt and pepper

Drain, flake and bone the salmon. Combine with all the other ingredients and mix well. Place in 6 well-greased muffin tins or custard cups set in hot water and bake for 45 minutes at 350° (gas mark 4). Serve with tartare sauce.

Salmon soufflé

4 tablespoons butter or margarine
4 tablespoons flour
1½ cups milk
1¾ cups salmon
1 teaspoon lemon juice
Salt and pepper
3 separated eggs

Melt the butter and blend with the flour. Gradually add the milk, stirring constantly and cook until smooth and thick. Add the fish and seasonings. Remove from the heat and add the beaten egg yolks, then mix and fold in the stiffly beaten egg whites. Grease the bottom only of a casserole. Turn the mixture into it and bake at 325° (gas mark 3) for 45 to 60 minutes or until an inserted knife comes out clean. Serve at once.

Salmon trout

A delicious fish. May be cooked like salmon and eaten hot or cold.

Braised salmon trout

Sauté a small carrot, a small onion and 1 stick of celery, all finely chopped, in 2 oz (50g) of butter or margarine until they begin to brown. Add a bouquet garni. Place the salmon trout in the dish, add ¼ pint (150ml) of red wine and ¼ pint of water, and cook for 35 to 40 minutes at 375° (gas mark 5).

The sauce: Reduce the cooking liquor by quick boiling to half. Make a roux of butter and flour, stir into the sauce and simmer for 3 minutes, beating well.

Skate

Skate must be skinned before being cooked. It may be steamed, fried, boiled or baked. To keep it in shape, roll and tie the pieces before boiling or steaming. Serve with any fish sauce or with black butter.

Sole

Sole is the aristocrat of flat fish. It may be fried or grilled whole. If large, it may be filletted and fried, or steamed or baked.

Grilled sole

Place sole fillets on a greased ovenproof dish. Spread lightly with anchovy paste and dot with butter. Sprinkle thickly with a mixture of equal quantities of crushed cornflakes, minced onion and cheese. Bake in a moderate oven at 350° (gas mark 4). The time will depend on the thickness of the fillets. To test for doneness, stick a toothpick into the thickest part of the fillet and separate the flakes; if the flesh is no longer translucent the fish is cooked. Serve with Hollandaise sauce.

Sole with cider sauce

1½ lb filletted sole (675g)
Paprika
¼ pint cider (150ml)

2 tablespoons butter or margarine
2 tablespoons flour
Salt and pepper
$\frac{1}{4}$ pint cream or top of bottle (150ml)
2 oz mushrooms (50g)

Place the fish in a shallow greased baking pan. If the fillets are large, cut them in half. Sprinkle with paprika. Pour the cider over them and bake in a moderate oven until just tender, basting now and then with the cider. Remove and keep hot.

Make a roux of butter and flour, and gradually add the liquid in which the fish was baked. Cook, stirring constantly, until the sauce is smooth and boiling. Reduce the heat and add seasoning and cream. Stir over a very low heat until the sauce is hot but do not allow it to boil. Add the sliced mushrooms which have been blanched in boiling water. Pour the sauce over the fillets and place them under the grill for a few minutes until the sauce is bubbly and lightly browned in spots.

Sole with tomatoes

1 lb fillets of sole (450g)
Salt and pepper
2 oz butter or margarine (50g)
8 oz sliced tomatoes (225g)
1 dessertspoonful flour
1 tablespoon chopped onion

Butter a fireproof dish, and put the rolled fillets into it. Sprinkle with seasoning and dot with 1 oz of the butter. Bake for about 15 minutes at 400° (gas mark 6). Stew the tomatoes (no water) until soft, and put them through a sieve. Knead the remainder of the butter to a paste with the flour. Combine with the tomatoes and onion and stir the sauce while it simmers, for about 5 minutes. Add any liquor from the fish. Pour the sauce over the fish and garnish with parsley.

Trout

Large trout are cooked like salmon. Small trout should be grilled, fried or baked.

Trout meunière
Wash, clean and dry the trout, roll in seasoned flour and fry golden brown in clarified butter. Place on a hot dish, sprinkle with chopped parsley and lemon juice and serve with a good helping of black butter.

Trout fried with mushrooms	**4 small trout** **2 oz flour (50g)** **4 oz butter or margarine (110g)** **4 oz mushrooms (110g)** **$\frac{1}{2}$ pint cream or half cream, half milk (275ml)** **Salt and pepper**

Clean, wash and dry the trout. Roll in 1 oz of the flour, seasoned with salt and pepper, and fry in 2 oz of the butter. Drain and keep hot. Cook the mushrooms in the fat in which the trout was fried. Melt the rest of the butter and blend in the flour. Add the milk or cream and season to taste. Add the mushrooms and reheat to serving point. Garnish with parsley and serve the sauce separately.

Whitebait

Bíonn blás ar an mbeagán (the morsel is always tasty) is a proverb that was inspired by whitebait. This fairy fish needs to be carefully dried before cooking. After washing and draining in a colander, pat the whitebait dry in a cloth. Sprinkle with seasoned flour, toss gently in a fish basket to remove surplus flour, then fry until crisp and delicately brown (about 3 minutes) in deep boiling fat. Serve with lemon slices and brown bread and butter.

Whiting

Whiting may be steamed or boiled and served with egg sauce or any favourite fish sauce.

To fry, skin and fasten the tail through the eye-holes. Dip in egg and breadcrumbs and fry in deep or shallow fat. Garnish with lemon and parsley.

Vegetables

The way Lottie Fenlon hated onions was a great hardship on Hugh Doherty.

'Miss Fenlon has agreed to take you as a boarder,' Father Molloy told Hugh when he first came to Ballyderrig to oversee the renovation of the Church. 'She's a grand cook. You'll be comfortable with her.'

At fifty, good cooking and comfort were very important to Hugh. Lottie bore out the priest's recommendation. In return for his two-ten a week, her boarder got a good fire, a good bed, a comfortable armchair and the pleasant companionship of his gentle-voiced landlady. Her soda bread was feather-light, her roasts dripped juice, and she had a way with sauces that could transform the most pallid bit of boiled cod into a fast-day feast.

For Hugh, her cooking had one big lack. She never used onions. Hugh was partial to onions. He liked them fried as his mother used to cook them. Not the grease-sodden discoloured strings which so many women pass off as fried onions, but those crisp golden-brown rings, tender and succulent, which you get if the rings are separated, tossed in seasoned flour or dipped in batter, then fried for three minutes in boiling fat.

There were few dishes he liked more than boiled onions, smothered in cheese sauce, topped with breadcrumbs and browned in the oven. He adored baby onions chopped small and added with hot milk and a lump of butter or margarine to fluffy mashed potatoes. Given his choice of supper-time sandwiches, he would swear that there was nothing to beat buttered wholemeal bread and thin slivers of Spanish onion, well-seasoned.

But Lottie would not let an onion into the house. The reason was psychological. Onions had been responsible for the wrecking of her first and only romance. It had happened twenty years before when she was seventeen and in love with a bank clerk called Cecil Quin, a very refined young man who would have died rather than be seen in the street without his yellow gloves and walking-stick.

Lottie's romance crashed the evening she had onions for tea before meeting Cecil for their bi-weekly walk along the canal bank. If Mrs. Fenlon had lived long enough to tell her daughter the facts of life, Lottie would have known that, provided proper precautions are taken, a girl may eat an acre of onions without fear of alienating her boy friend, however refined. She would have been taught that a glass of milk sipped slowly or a mouthful of parsley chewed leisurely will destroy all evidence of onion-eating.

But poor Lottie was an uninstructed orphan. When, on that fateful evening, Cecil bent to give her one of his carefully rationed kisses, she was hurt and dismayed to see him rear back offendedly. He left her with a quick good-night and never took her out again. A year later he married Angela Murphy, who was as refined as himself and who had a good dowry into the bargain. To complete Lottie's humiliation, Angela told all Ballyderrig of the solecism that had killed the bank clerk's love. From that day Lottie turned her back on men and on onions.

After Hugh came to board with her, he made a few tentative suggestions regarding the culinary uses of onions ... that though steak was good with mushrooms, it was even better with onion rings ... that stuffing was not the same, somehow, without onions.

Lottie froze him. 'If you want onions, Mr. Doherty,' she said, her voice trembling, 'I'm afraid you will have to find accommodation elsewhere. Inside this door an onion will never come!'

After that, he put up with the lack of his favourite vegetable, feeling that Lottie's house afforded compensations which atoned. She was glad he stayed. Since his coming she had discovered that a woman who lives alone can be very lonely.

When he had been with her about three months, Lottie had to go to Dublin to see about a tooth that was worrying her. 'I won't be able to get a bus back until the morning,' she told him. 'If I leave you to look after yourself for the night, will you be all right?'

Hugh assured her that he could manage. Just the same, she was worried. When she walked into Father Molloy in Dublin that evening, she was glad to accept his offer of a lift home.

When she stepped into her beeswaxed hall, she stopped dead and sniffed. There was no mistaking the smell. Onions were being cooked in her kitchen!

She threw open the kitchen door. There was Mr. Doherty, one of her aprons tied around his ample middle, happily engaged in basting something that sent its aroma through the house. At her step, he turned quickly and dropped the spoon. Guilt and dismay made his flushed face several shades redder.

'I'm – I'm sorry,' he stammered, hanging his head. 'I – I was making stuffed onions the way my mother used to do them.'

There was something in the big man's apologetic humility, in the disarray of his wispy fair hair and in his scared blue eyes which awoke latent maternalism in Lottie Fenlon. All at once, the anger left her. The bitterness of years went from her. It was replaced by something soft and warm which make her look ten years younger.

Hugh Doherty saw the transformation. In some peculiar way, it made him stop feeling like a schoolboy caught stealing apples. Instead, he felt like a masterful man. He acted like one too. In two strides he was across the kitchen and had Lottie in his arms.

For their betrothal supper they ate the stuffed onions. Luckily, Hugh had cooked enough for two.

In addition to boiling, methods of cooking vegetables include simmering, steaming, broiling and baking. Steaming is a good way of cooking most vegetables. A steamer cooks without added moisture and prevents loss of minerals. Vegetables which are baked in a casserole and served in the same dish at the table retain all the materials. The next time you bake a joint, just try baking in the tin with it any of the root vegetables such as turnips and parsnips. Not only will you be sure of retaining all the nutriment, but you'll find the flavour of the vegetables a hundred per cent better than when boiled.

For cooking purposes, vegetables are generally grouped according to colour ... green, yellow, white and red. The green vegetables include all leafy vegetables, and green beans, peas, broccoli and sprouts. The green colour is partially soluble in water and is destroyed by long cooking and by the presence of acid. Bread soda should never be added to vegetables — it destroys their most valuable nutrients. Cook green vegetables as quickly as possible, and with as little water as possible. Leafy vegetables are best boiled. Steaming is too slow for them.

Water and heat do not affect the colour of yellow vegetables. They may be cooked, covered, in a small amount of water, or they may be steamed, or braised, or baked. The white vegetables include such varieties as Savoy cabbage, onions, potatoes, leeks and cauliflower. These are particularly liable to become strong-flavoured if overcooked. Use any one of the five methods for cooking them.

At this point it might be well to discuss briefly the foibles and idiosyncrasies of the various kinds of vegetables. If I treat the subject with a certain seriousness, it is because I feel it merits serious treatment. Here in Ireland, we are apt to be far too casual and light-hearted in our way of dealing with vegetables. There may be an excuse for us. Until comparatively recently, the majority of us , in country parts anyway, grew or knew very few vegetables beyond potatoes, cabbage and turnips. And maybe this is why so many of us even in this day or hour treat every vegetable as if it were one of the three I have mentioned and subject it to the unvarying formula: 'Boil it until it is soft and serve it mashed.'

Since incorrect cooking so often destroys the valuable constituents of vegetables, it may be asked: Why cook them at all? The answer is: To increase palatability. Many vegetables increase in flavour and digestibility when the starch is cooked and the cellulose is broken down.

And now for the red vegetables: These are the common or garden beetroot and red cabbage. Tomatoes which, like cucumbers, belong to what are known as fruit vegetables, do not come under this heading. Both beetroot and red cabbage are liable to go pale in water. This is particularly so in the case of beetroot, which is why this vegetable is always cooked with its skin and stem ends. Red cabbage should be boiled. Beetroot may be baked or simmered.

Artichokes (globe)

For each person allow 1 large or 2 small artichokes. Wash under the cold tap, taking care that water reaches inside the petals (artichokes are inclined to be gritty). With scissors, remove petal points, trimming crown down evenly. Cook in a saucepan large enough to hold the artichokes in one layer. Stand, base down, in a saucepan. Add boiling salted water, almost to cover. Cook, covered, until tender (from 20 to 45 minutes according to size). Drain, upside down. Serve hot with melted butter or Hollandaise sauce, or serve cold with French dressing.

Artichokes (Jerusalem)

This root vegetable deserves to figure more often on the menu. But it needs care in cooking. If artichokes are allowed to continue cooking after they have become tender, they are liable to become tough again. Wash and peel the artichokes and drop them into boiling water. Cook them, covered, until they are tender. After 15 minutes test with a toothpick. Drain them and keep them in a hot place while you prepare the following dressing: Melt 2 tablespoons of butter or margarine. Add 1 teaspoon mild white vinegar or dry white wine, and 2 teaspoons of chopped parsley. Pour this dressing over the artichokes and serve at once.

Creamed artichokes

Cook the artichokes as in preceding recipe. Drain them well

and pour over them enough cream sauce to make a good topping — about ½ pint (275ml) of cream sauce to 1½ lb (675g) of artichokes. Sprinkle thickly with chopped parsley.

Asparagus

Scrape, trim stalks and tie in bundles. Place, standing upright, in a saucepan. Add boiling water to come just below the tips. Boil (uncovered) for 10 to 20 minutes, according to size. Then place the bundles on their side, and cook gently until tender. Drain, and serve with melted butter or Hollandaise sauce.

Aubergine (egg plant)

Usually eaten baked, plain with a sauce, or stuffed. If you find the taste slightly bitter, sprinkle them liberally with salt and put them in a colander with a weighted plate on top. Within half an hour a lot of surplus water will have drained off. Rinse and dry in a cloth.

Baked aubergines

Peel and slice the aubergines. Place them in a greased fireproof dish, dot with butter, and season with salt and pepper. Cover and bake at 400° (gas mark 6) for 20 minutes. Sprinkle with grated cheese or breadcrumbs and bake for another 10 minutes, until browned. Serve with sauce.

Stuffed aubergines

Cut the aubergines in two lengthwise. Make a cavity by scooping out a little of the centre. Chop the removed portion finely, and mix with a stuffing made with 8 oz (225g) of minced meat, mixed herbs, ½ clove of crushed garlic, chopped parsley and seasoning. Pack the stuffing into the cavities. Place the halved aubergines on a baking sheet, brush with melted butter and bake at 375° (gas mark 5) for 45 minutes.

Avocado

Usually eaten raw, as a hors d'oeuvre. To prepare, cut through the avocado to the stone and twist to separate the halves. Run a sharp knife down the centre back of each half, cutting through the thin outer rind only. Peel off each section of skin. Slice, and sprinkle liberally with lemon juice to prevent darkening.

Beans (French and runner)

Early summer while they are young, juicy and tender is the time to enjoy French and runner beans. You need not even string them — just trim off the stalks and tips. You may cook them whole, or cut into 1-inch lengths, or you may sliver them lengthwise, French fashion.

For French beans at their very best, cook them the 'conservative way', i.e., with a minimum of water. Add ½ to 1 inch boiling salted water, cover closely and cook until tender but not mushy — 15 to 20 minutes for whole beans or 1-inch lengths; 10 minutes for strips. The slight amount of liquid left in the saucepan when the beans are cooked should be drained off and used in gravy or sauce.

To preserve beans

Beans — whether French or runner — may be preserved very successfully in salt. The secret of success is to use enough salt (1 lb of salt to 3 lb of beans is about right) and to use only young tender beans. A large earthenware crock or glass jar will be needed. String the beans, but do not wash them. See that the jar is clean and dry. Put a layer of salt in the bottom of the jar. Set aside about ½ lb of salt and mix the remainder with the beans. Press them down really well in the jar and cover with a layer of salt. The pressing down is important, since the more tightly packed the beans the better they will keep. That is why it is better not to cover and store the jar right away. Leave it for 3 or 4 days, when it will be found that the beans will bear further pressing down. Add more salted beans so that the jar is tightly packed, and cover these with another layer of salt. Cover the jar with several layers of brown paper and store in a cool dark place.

To use: Wash beans in several lots of cold water, and then

soak them for 2 hours in warm water. Rinse and cook in the usual way, but without adding salt to the cooking water. They will taste like fresh beans.

Beans with mushroom sauce
Mix 1 lb cooked French beans with 1 tin undiluted cream of mushroom soup. Place in a baking dish. Top with buttered crumbs or crisp French fried onions (onion rings dipped in batter and fried in deep fat). Bake for 12 minutes in a moderate oven.

Beans Parisienne
Prepare 1 lb beans by cutting in thin diagonal slices. When cooked, simmer for 3 minutes in a sauce made as follows: Melt 2oz (50g) of butter in a heavy saucepan. Add 1 teaspoon lemon juice, salt, and cayenne to taste and 2 tablespoons water or liquid in which the beans were cooked. Serve very hot.

Beans and potatoes
This is a Spanish dish called *hervido*. Cook until tender in boiling salted water equal quantities of new potatoes and French beans. Drain and toss in a generous amount of French dressing. Serve hot.

Beans and tomatoes
To 1 lb (450g) of cooked French beans add 1 cup of tomato purée made as follows: Melt 2oz (50g) of butter or bacon fat over a low heat. Add 8 oz chopped ripe tomatoes, 1 dessertspoon parsley, 1 tablespoon minced onion and pepper and salt to taste. Cover closely and simmer until the tomatoes are tender. Force through a sieve. Add the purée to the hot beans and heat thoroughly.

Devilled beans
Combine 2 teaspoons prepared mustard, 2 teaspoons sugar, 2oz (50g) of butter or margarine and $\frac{1}{2}$ teaspoon salt. Heat slowly, stirring constantly. Stir in 2 teaspoons of lemon juice and 2 teaspoons of vinegar. Add to this sauce 1lb (450g) of cooked green beans. Heat thoroughly.

Hungarian beans

Place 1 lb (450g) of cooked French beans in a large baking dish. Mix together 2 cups medium cream sauce, 1 tablespoon minced onion, 2 teaspoons minced parsley, $\frac{1}{4}$ teaspoon paprika, salt and pepper to taste, 2 egg yolks, slightly beaten, and 2oz sautéed mushrooms. Pour this sauce over the beans. Top with buttered crumbs and bake for 30 minutes at 350° (gas mark 4).

Viennese beans

Cook $1\frac{1}{2}$ lb (675g) of French beans cut in thin strips. Drain. Melt 1 tablespoon of butter and stir in 1 tablespoon of flour. Add 1 teaspoon minced parsley, 2 tablespoons minced onion and stir in gradually 3 tablespoons (45ml) of the liquid in which the beans were cooked. Stir until smooth and slightly thickened. Season to taste and add 2 tablespoons of sour cream and 1 teaspoon of vinegar. Pour this sauce over the beans and serve hot.

Beetroot

Sliced or diced beetroot, either cold or hot, is a delicious and valuable vegetable. Carefully remove any little roots, about an inch away from the skin. Leave on the stalk. Wash gently and without breaking the skin and plunge into plenty of boiling salted water containing a little vinegar. Cover and simmer steadily until tender. If the beets are young, allow about an hour's cooking. If old, allow two hours or more.

Drain and peel carefully with the blunt edge of a knife. Cut into thick slices or dice. If the beetroot is to be served hot, season to taste with pepper and hot vinegar and moisten with melted butter. A minced fried onion added gives a delicious flavour. If the beetroot is to be served cold, do not slice until just before serving.

Broad beans

Boiled beans

Pod the beans, wash and place in a saucepan with $\frac{1}{2}$ inch of boiling salted water. Cook until tender. Drain, and serve with minced parsley and melted butter.

With parsley sauce

Cook beans as in the preceding recipe. Drain and place in a serving dish. Mask with parsley sauce. Broad beans are also good with tomato purée.

To dry beans and peas

To dry peas or beans, shell and parboil them. Peas should be given 5 minutes in boiling salted water. Beans take 7 minutes. Then drain and pat off the surplus moisture with a dry cloth. They should then be spread on wire cake trays lined with muslin — or on drying trays made by nailing four laths in a square and stretching muslin over this frame. Put the vegetables in a cool oven and leave them until they are parched and dry. Be sure to leave the oven door open. The drying will take about 12 hours — sometimes more.

When taken out of the oven the beans should be 'sweated' — that is, left at room temperature for another 12 hours or so. After the twelve hours, put them in paper bags, tie securely and hang up in a cool airy place. It is wise to examine them from time to time in case one or two should not have been absolutely dry and should have gone 'mitey'. Any in this condition should be removed. And to make assurance doubly sure, spread the remaining peas from the bag on a tray and leave in the sun for an hour or two, after which they may be packed in a fresh bag and hung up as before. Before using, the vegetables must be steeped overnight.

Broccoli

Remove the green leaves and trim the sprigs from the stalks. Tie the sprigs in bundles and cook in boiling salted water to cover for 15 minutes. Serve sprinkled with buttered brown crumbs, or with melted butter or with cheese or cream sauce.

The sprigs of broccoli may be left on the stalk, which is very good to eat. In this case, slit the stalk across at the stump and cook the broccoli for 5 minutes longer.

Brussels sprouts

These, more than any other vegetable, seem fated to be over-cooked. Trim the stalks, remove withered leaves and soak for 15 minutes in cold salted water. Drain well and cook (uncovered) in boiling salted water for about 15 minutes or until barely tender. Drain, sprinkle with melted butter and pepper and salt.

Butter beans

Bean casserole

Soak the beans overnight, then cook them until tender in the water in which they were soaked. Cook three sliced carrots until tender and sauté, with a sliced onion, in 1 oz (25g) of butter or margarine for a few minutes. Combine with the butter beans, season and stir until very hot. Serve in a casse-role.

Boiled beans

Soak 4 oz (110g) of dried butter beans overnight in plenty of cold water. Next day, drain and put into a saucepan with 1 pint (570ml) of cold water, a sliced onion, and a teaspoon of salt. Cover and simmer until tender (about 2 hours). Drain and toss in melted butter. Season to taste and sprinkle with parsley.

Cabbage

Overcooking, the use of soda, and too much cooking water are three factors which destroy the food value of cabbage. To pre-serve nutrients and flavour, try cooking cabbage as follows:

Cut the cabbage in halves lengthwise, then into quarters. Discard woody parts and damaged outer leaves — but only the *damaged* outer leaves: remember that the darker leaves contain more vitamin A. Shred the cabbage and wash well in cold water.

Into a saucepan which will just contain the cabbage put not more than $\frac{1}{2}$ inch of boiling water. Add salt (about $\frac{1}{2}$ teaspoon to 1 pint of water). When the water is boiling, put in the cabbage. Cover with a well-fitting lid and boil fast for about 10 minutes. Stir the cabbage at intervals to turn it over in the saucepan, and add a little more water if there is danger of it boiling dry. The cabbage is cooked when it is tender, but firm. There should be very little water to drain off. What there is, use for stock. Toss the cabbage in a little melted margarine, butter or bacon fat and season to taste with salt and pepper. Sometime, try adding a little grated nutmeg and/or lemon juice.

Cabbage rolls
Wash 4 large cabbage leaves (not too coarse). Mix together 6 oz (175g) of minced meat, 1 dessertspoon chopped onion, 2 oz breadcrumbs and season to taste. Bind with a little stock or beaten egg. Divide the mince mixture into four, and lay on the cabbage leaves. Roll up and tie with string.

Place the stuffed cabbage leaves in a saucepan, in one layer. Add stock or water to a depth of $\frac{1}{2}$ inch. Cover the saucepan and simmer gently for 15 minutes. Remove the rolls on to a platter and keep in a warm place. In a saucepan, melt 1 tablespoon of butter or margarine. Blend with this $1\frac{1}{2}$ tablespoons of flour and stir over a gentle heat until light brown. Add the stock in which the cabbage rolls were cooked, together with additional water or stock to make $\frac{1}{2}$ pint (275ml). Season to taste and add 1 teaspoon yeast extract. Pour the sauce over the rolls and serve with boiled or mashed potatoes.

Cabbage with tomato and cheese
Cook about 3 cups of finely shredded cabbage for 5 minutes and drain well. Skin and slice 8 oz (225g) of tomatoes. Season with salt and pepper and add 1 teaspoon of brown sugar. Cook until tender in about 1 cup of the cabbage water.

Butter a baking dish. Place in it alternate layers of tomatoes and cabbage, beginning with tomatoes. Sprinkle the layers with 3 oz (75g) of grated cheese mixed with 3 oz (75g) of breadcrumbs. Dot the top with 2 streaky rashers, chopped small. Bake for about 30 minutes at 325° (gas mark 3) or until the crumbs are brown.

Cabbage and tomato pie

Skin and slice 8 oz (225g) tomatoes and simmer until soft in
about 1 tablespoon of butter or margarine. Season with salt
and pepper, and add 1 teaspoon of brown sugar. Shred finely
the heart of 1 large cabbage (there should be about 3 breakfastcups). Cook in boiling salted water for not more than 6
minutes, or until it is tender but still crisp.

Place alternate layers of cabbage and stewed tomatoes in a
buttered pie dish, sprinkling the layers with a mixture of
grated cheese and breadcrumbs (about 1 tablespoon of each to
each layer). Finish with a layer of crumbs and cheese. Dot the
top with butter and bake for about 25 minutes at 350° (gas
mark 4).

Stuffed cabbage

Separate the leaves of a large cabbage. Wash and cook,
uncovered, for 5 minutes in boiling water. Drain the cabbage
well and reserve the liquor. Prepare the following stuffing:
Soak a thick slice of bread in stock or water for two minutes.
Press the water from the bread and combine it with 8 oz (225g)
of minced steak, 8 oz (225g) of sausage meat, a beaten egg, 1
tablespoon of minced onion, salt and pepper.

Line a greased bowl with alternate layers of cabbage leaves
and meat mixture. Top it with 1 or 2 large leaves. Tie down
with greased paper, and steam for 1 hour. Turn out on a hot
dish and serve with onion sauce.

Red cabbage, baked

Wash and shred a head of red cabbage — there should be
about 1 lb (450g). Mix with 4 oz (110g) of diced streaky bacon
and put into a greased casserole. Sprinkle with pepper and dot
with butter or margarine. Cover closely and let the cabbage
cook in its own steam until tender (about 1 hour) at 350° (gas
mark 4).

Cauliflower

Boiled cauliflower

Cut the cauliflower through the stem end into halves and then into quarters. Discard only rough outside leaves. Cut away the woody part of the stump and place upside down in a saucepan. Add about $\frac{1}{2}$ inch boiling salted water, cover tightly and cook rapidly for about 15 minutes. When cooked, sprinkle with melted butter and crumbs. Or serve with medium cream sauce.

Cauliflower cheese
Place cooked cauliflower in a casserole, cover with cheese sauce and top with crumbs and grated cheese. Dot with butter and place under the grill or in a hot oven until golden-brown.

Carrots
In the advance guard of the summer vegetables come the first carrots, chubby and tender and very sweet. Dieticians teach that it is murder to subject these harbingers of the garden's gifts to any form of cooking. Eaten raw in salads (or nibbled between meals) they retain all their goodness. And this goodness includes protein, calcium, phosphorus, iron, vitamin A, thiamin, ribo-flavin, niacin and ascorbic acid. Boil carrots in the usual way and their value is lost in the cooking water.

If you feel you must cook your carrots, use as little water as possible. When tender, let them stand over a low heat until they have absorbed all the cooking water.

Buttered carrots
Wash the carrots, trim them and place, sliced or whole, in a small quantity of boiling water. Cook (covered) until they are tender and leave over a moderate heat until the cooking water is absorbed. Add salt to taste. Now add a couple of tablespoons of melted butter and a generous sprinkling of finely chopped parsley. Toss the carrots until they are well coated and serve hot.

Whole buttered baby carrots are excellent served with roast meat. Serve in two bunches, one at each end of the meat dish. Place sprigs of parsley at the blunt ends of the carrots to represent carrot greens.

Carrots creamed au gratin

Boil 2 cups of carrots, sliced or whole. Prepare 1 cup of cream sauce and combine with the cooked carrots. Place in a greased baking dish. Cover with breadcrumbs, dot with 2 tablespoons of butter and sprinkle with 3 tablespoons of grated cheese. Bake in a hot oven or place under the grill until the top is golden-brown.

Carrot ring

This is a nice way of combining new peas and young carrots. Served with poached eggs, it makes a good and well-balanced meal.

Cook the carrots until tender, then put them through a ricer or mash them. Beat in 1 tablespoon of butter, salt and pepper, and 1 tablespoon of chopped parsley or chives. Arrange in a ring on a large dish and fill the centre with green peas flavoured with mint.

Glazed French carrots

Place in a saucepan about 2 cups of sliced washed carrots. Add ½ cup of boiling water, 2 tablespoons butter, 1 tablespoon sugar, salt and pepper. Cover the pan closely and cook over a quick heat until the water evaporates. Allow the carrots to brown in the butter — but over a low heat; otherwise, the sugar and butter may carmelize. Sprinkle with chopped chives or parsley and serve hot.

Macedoine of spring carrot

Boil about 2 cups of sliced young carrots with 8 or 9 chopped scallions, including the green parts. When cooked, mix with them a cup of green peas. Add 3 tablespoons of melted butter, and pepper and salt to taste. Serve sprinkled with chopped parsley.

Celeriac

Wash and peel 2 heads of celeriac. Cut into cubes, and simmer in boiling salted water until tender. Add a good knob of butter and shake until melted and absorbed. Celeriac can also be mashed with butter.

Celery

Boiled celery

Trim off the green ends, cut off the root, split and wash carefully to free from sandy soil and insects. Cut into small or long lengths and cook, in sufficient boiling water to cover, until tender.

Braised celery

Prepare as for boiled celery but cut into long lengths. Parboil for a few minutes (the length of time will depend on how young the celery is), then cool in cold water, drain and tie in bundles.

In the bottom of a casserole put some sliced onions, carrots and a bouquet garni, and line the sides with thin slices of bacon. Lay the celery in the casserole and sweat in the oven for about 10 minutes with the lid on. Add sufficient stock to come half way up the casserole, and cook for about 45 minutes at 450° (gas mark 8). Strain off the stock into a saucepan, and add 1 oz (25g) of butter into which you have worked 1 oz (25g) of flour. Bring to boil and simmer for 3 minutes. Serve very hot, with the sauce poured over.

If the sauce is too pale, colour with a little browning or yeast extract.

Celery au gratin

Cook as for boiled celery. Place in a casserole, cover with cheese sauce, top with breadcrumbs and grated cheese, and dot with butter. Brown in a very hot oven or under the grill.

Stuffed celery

Use only the crisp, tender white stalks of a head of celery. Wash and leave the tips of the leaves on the stalks. Dry well before stuffing with 2 finely minced hard-boiled eggs bound with about 4 tablespoons of mayonnaise and seasoned with salt and pepper. Sprinkle lightly with chopped parsley. Excellent served with cold meat or fish.

Chicory

Wash 1 lb (450g) of chicory to remove any sand. Place the pieces side by side in a saucepan. Add 2 oz (50g) of butter, 3 or

4 tablespoons of stock, a little lemon juice, salt and pepper. Cover tightly, bring to the boil and simmer gently for 20 minutes. Serve with the cooking liquor.

Endive

A plant of the lettuce family, endive is usually used raw in salad, but may be served braised, as chicory, or with sour cream sauce.

Haricot beans

Beans à la Bretonne

Wash 8 oz (225g) of haricot beans and soak overnight in about 5 times their weight of water. Next day, simmer the beans until tender in the water in which they were soaked. Drain and keep hot.

Make a stock for the sauce by simmering 4 oz (110g) of chopped carrots, two tablespoons of chopped onion and ½ teaspoon of mixed herbs in about 1 pint (570ml) of water for 30 minutes. Reduce by rapid boiling to about ½ pint (275ml). Sauté about 6 oz (175g) of chopped onions in butter or margarine until brown, add 1 dessertspoon of flour and brown it lightly, then 1 dessertspoon of tomato sauce and mix well. Now, work in the stock gradually, stirring constantly. Bring to the boil and cook for 2 minutes. Pour over the cooked beans and serve very hot.

Buttered beans

Soak 8 oz (225g) of beans overnight. Next day cover with cold salted water, add 2 small sliced onions, bring to the boil, skim, and add a small amount of butter or margarine. Cover and simmer for 2 hours or until tender. Drain, toss in melted butter and stir in 1 dessertspoon of chopped parsley. Season and serve hot.

Drying herbs: All culinary herbs except parsley may be preserved. Tie in bunches, wrap in butter muslin and hang in a dry room. After three weeks they will be ready for storing. Rub the leaves from the stems (bay leaves should be left whole) and store in dry airtight tins or jars.

Kolhrabi

Peel and cube 1 kohlrabi root. Cook rapidly in boiling salted water until tender. Use the water to make a cream sauce.

Leeks

Boiled leeks

Leeks look and taste best when cooked whole. Trim the root and part of the tops, allowing about 2 inches of green to remain. Wash well under running water to remove the sandy soil which usually clings to leeks. Cover with not more than 1 inch of boiling water, and boil until tender. Drain well, season with salt and paprika and serve with melted butter.

Braised leeks

Follow the recipe for braised celery.

Leeks au gratin

Clean and trim 6 or 8 leeks and cut them into 1 inch lengths, using only the white and yellowish-green parts. Wash well, cook (uncovered) in boiling water until tender, and drain.

Prepare about ¾ pint (425ml) of cream sauce, and when it is cooked stir into it 3 tablespoons of grated cheese. Place half of the leeks in a shallow buttered baking dish and cover with half of the sauce. Add the remaining leeks and cover with the rest of the sauce. Dot with butter, sprinkle thickly with breadcrumbs and brown in a moderately hot oven.

Stuffed leeks

Prepare 12 large leeks, using only the white tops — they should be about 3 inches long. Parboil or steam them, then slit and take out the centres.

Make a stuffing with the finely chopped centres, 2 tablespoons of chopped carrot, 1 chopped hard-boiled egg, a teaspoon of parsley, season and bind with a beaten egg. Fill the leeks with this mixture. Lay them carefully in a greased pie dish, cover with cream sauce, sprinkle thickly with grated cheese and breadcrumbs and brown in a moderately hot oven.

Note: If the leeks are very sandy, split lengthwise and fan out under running water.

Lentils

A highly nutritious and inexpensive vegetable which does not appear half often enough on Irish menus.

Lentil loaf

8 oz red lentils (225g)
2 medium chopped onions
1 oz butter or margarine (25g)
1 pint stock (570ml)
8 oz mashed potatoes (225g)
4 oz breadcrumbs (110g)
1 dessertspoon chopped parsley
Salt and pepper

Wash the lentils and drain. Melt the butter, add the onion and lentils and stir for 5 minutes over a gentle heat. Add the stock, bring to the boil, cover and simmer gently until the lentils are soft. If necessary, more stock can be added but the lentils should be fairly dry when cooked. Drain off any surplus liquid, add the mashed potatoes, breadcrumbs, parsley and seasoning. Mix well together, put into a well-greased baking pan, dot with butter and bake, basting frequently, at 375° (gas mark 5) until nicely browned. Serve with a good brown gravy or tomato sauce.

Lentil rissoles

Using the same mixture as for the loaf, shape with floured hands into croquettes or patties. Dip in beaten egg, then in fine breadcrumbs and fry until golden-brown.

Note: Lentils are excellent with game. Boil until soft, cover with streaky rashers and bake in the oven.

Marrow

I agree with Philip Harben when he says that the overgrown marrow which wins prizes at shows should be regarded as a horticultural freak. Certainly the kitchen is no place for this tough and tasteless monstrosity. Its insipidity is responsible for the distaste with which many people view what can be a delicious vegetable — if cooked while it is small, young and tender. Here are recipes which will convert even the most rabid marrow-hater, always provided that you select a marrow which is not more than 12 inches long, with a skin so soft that it may be punctured by a fork.

Boiled marrow with cheese sauce

Peel the marrow, discard the seeds and cut into cubes. Simmer the marrow until tender in about $\frac{1}{2}$ pint (275ml) of boiling salted water. Place in a casserole, cover with cheese sauce and top with a mixture of $1\frac{1}{2}$ tablespoons of breadcrumbs and $1\frac{1}{2}$ tablespoons of grated cheese. Place under the grill or in a moderate oven until golden brown.

Stuffed marrow

Halve the marrow, remove the seeds and cut the halves into two pieces. Parboil for 10 minutes in boiling salted water, drain and arrange half in the bottom of a greased dish. Spread hamburger mixture on top, and cover with the rest of the marrow. Add $\frac{1}{2}$ pint (275ml) of brown gravy, cover and bake for 1 hour at 350° (gas mark 4).

Marrow can also be stuffed with sage and onion stuffing, veal or any savoury forcemeat.

Mushrooms

Broiled mushrooms

Select large cup mushrooms. Brush lightly with melted fat or oil and place, cap side down, on a hot greased broiler. Bake for $2\frac{1}{2}$ minutes on each side, turning once. Place a piece of butter in each mushroom, sprinkle with salt and pepper, chopped parsley and lemon juice.

Creamed mushrooms

Sauté 1 lb (450g) of mushrooms, and when moist and tender sprinkle with 2 tablespoons of flour. Add 1 cup of rich milk or stock and bring to the boil. Simmer for 3 minutes, then season with salt and pepper. Sherry, herbs, minced chives or parsley — any or all of these will improve the flavour. Makes a delicious supper with baked potatoes.

Mushroom platter

On a shallow fireproof dish arrange a ring of mashed potatoes.

Mix 2 cups of diced cooked meat or flaked cooked fish with a tin of cream of mushroom soup thinned with ½ cup of milk. Place the mixture in the potato ring and sprinkle with buttered crumbs (crumbs fried until crisp in butter or bacon fat). Brush the potatoes with beaten egg and bake at 400° (gas mark 6).

Mushroom stock

Put 1 cup of mushroom stems and skins, a small minced onion, a couple of sticks of celery, a medium chopped carrot and a dessertspoonful of parsley into a saucepan, and cover with 1¼ pints (720ml) of water. Simmer for 30 minutes and strain. Season with salt and pepper when ready to use. A tablespoonful of sherry makes a big difference to the flavour.

Sautéed mushrooms

Rub the pan with a clove of garlic, and sauté 1 lb (450g) of mushrooms in 2 tablespoons of butter or margarine for about 5 minutes. Season and add ¼ teaspoon of lemon juice. Very good with steak, hamburgers or fried bacon, or on toast.

Stewed mushrooms

Rub 8 oz (225g) of mushrooms with a cloth dipped in salt. Blend 2 oz (50g) of butter with 1 oz (25g) of flour and stir in ½ pint (275ml) of milk to make a sauce. Add the mushrooms and simmer gently until they are tender. Remove from the heat, add 2 tablespoons of cream and serve with triangles of buttered toast.

Stuffed mushrooms

Fill broiled mushrooms with a stuffing made with 1 cup of chopped mushroom stems and 1 tablespoon of chopped onion. Sauté lightly in butter or oil, then add ½ cup of breadcrumbs and ¼ teaspoon of dried herbs. Season, put the stuffing into the mushroom caps and reheat under the broiler.

Onions

Those who find that the king of vegetables does not agree with them should blanch the onions before cooking them. This will get rid of the sometimes upsetting volatile oils. Cover the sliced onions with boiling water, leave for 10 minutes, then drain and cook.

Devilled onions

Peel 6 large onions, cover with cold water, bring to the boil and simmer for 30 minutes or until tender. Drain and chop finely, and add the mashed yolks of 3 hard-boiled eggs, $1\frac{1}{2}$ tablespoons of chopped parsley, and $\frac{1}{2}$ pint (275ml) of medium white sauce. Season, turn into a greased casserole, sprinkle thickly with breadcrumbs, dot with butter and brown under the grill or in the top of the oven.

French fried onions

Peel 4 large onions and cut into $\frac{1}{4}$-inch slices. Separate into rings, soak for 30 minutes in milk and dip into seasoned flour. Fry in hot fat until lightly brown (6 to 8 minutes). Drain on absorbent paper before serving.

Fritter onions

Dip thinly sliced onions in pancake batter. Fry in deep fat for about 6 minutes and drain on absorbent paper.

Glazed onions

Wash and peel $1\frac{1}{2}$ lb (675g) of small white onions. Melt 2 tablespoons of butter or margarine in a frying-pan, add the onions, 4 tablespoons (60ml) of water and 1 tablespoon of sugar. Season and simmer gently for about 15 minutes or until tender. Blend 1 tablespoon of flour with 2 tablespoons of water and add to the onions. Turn into a casserole, cover and bake for 20 minutes at 375° (gas mark 5).

Onions Mornay

Simmer 4 medium-sized sliced onions in salted water until tender. Place a mound of buttered carrots in the centre of a dish, put the drained onions around them, surround the onions with a circle of sliced hard-boiled egg, and complete with a border of mashed potatoes. Cover with a good layer of cheese sauce and bake in a moderate oven until hot.

Onion and tomato casserole

Simmer 4 large onions in boiling salted water for 30 minutes.

Drain and cut into quarters. Slice 1 lb (450g) of tomatoes thickly. Grease a casserole, sprinkle with 1 oz (25g) of fine brown crumbs and add the onions and tomatoes. Season, top with brown crumbs and dot with 2 oz (50g) of butter or margarine and bake for 35 minutes at 375° (gas mark 5).

Stuffed onions
Simmer 6 large onions for 5 minutes. Drain and take out the centres. Chop them finely, and mix with 4 tablespoons of breadcrumbs, 1 tablespoon of melted butter or margarine, the well-beaten yolk of an egg, 1 teaspoon of chopped parsley, $\frac{1}{2}$ teaspoon of dried herbs, salt and pepper. Fill the onions with this mixture, place in a saucepan, add 1 pint (570ml) of brown gravy or stock, cover and simmer for 2 hours. Take out carefully and place on a warm dish. Thicken the gravy with a little *beurre manié*, boil and pour around the onions.

Parsnips

Baked parsnips
Parboil parsnips. About 20 minutes before the roast is cooked, place them in the baking tin beside the meat. Baste well.

Boiled parsnips
Parsnips for boiling should be young and medium sized. If small, leave whole and unscraped. If large, scrape and cut into quarters lengthwise, or slice or dice. Cook in boiling salted water until tender. Drain, mash or leave whole, season and dress with melted butter. A squeeze of lemon juice adds zest.

Parsnips can also be served with any of the usual vegetable sauces — cream, parsley or cheese.

Peas

If you grow your own peas you score over the rest of us who must accept the greengrocer's word as to freshness. The flavour of green peas depends on their freshness. Whether from garden or shop, peas should not be hulled until just before cooking.

Peas should be cooked with barely sufficient water to keep them from burning. When very young, the peas will be cooked almost as soon as the water boils up. As they grow older, they may take anything from 1 to 5 minutes. To cook them longer is to spoil them. Peas combine well with other vegetables, as these recipes prove.

Note: 1 lb of peas in the pod will yield about 1 cup of hulled peas (2 servings).

Bonne femme peas

Sauté 12 spring onions (white part only) and 4 oz (110g) of streaky bacon in 2 oz (50g) of butter until tender. Add 2 lb (900g) of shelled peas, a quartered lettuce head, 1 teaspoon of sugar and a small cup of boiling water, cover and cook until the peas are tender. Sprinkle in sufficient flour to thicken the mixture (about 1 dessertspoon), and cook for another 3 minutes. Season with pepper and, if bacon is very mild, a little salt. Serve with triangles of toast.

Creamed peas

Melt 2 oz (50g) of butter, add 1 cup of spring onions (white part only), cover and cook over moderate heat until they are tender. Add 2 lb (900g) of shelled peas, 1 teaspoon of sugar, salt and pepper, and 4 tablespoons (60ml) of water, and continue to cook until the peas are tender. Add 6 tablespoons (90ml) of cream and stir over a low heat until hot.

With hard-boiled eggs and boiled potatoes, this makes an excellent meal.

Peas and lettuce

Put 2 lb (900g) of peas in the top of a double saucepan, with the leaves from 2 heads of lettuce. Cover and steam until the peas are cooked. Remove the lettuce leaves, chop finely, season with salt and a little butter, and shape into a border on a hot dish. Season the peas, add some butter and serve in the border of lettuce, sprinkled with chopped parsley.

Peas and mushrooms

Cook 2 lb (900g) of peas in boiling water. Drain and reserve the liquor. Melt 2 tablespoons of butter or margarine in a frying-pan, add 1 lb (450g) of sliced mushrooms, and cook slowly until tender. Remove the mushrooms, and to the fat in the pan add 1 tablespoon of flour. Stir and cook slowly as it bubbles. Combine and stir in slowly ½ cup of liquor from the peas and 3 tablespoons (45ml) of cream or top of bottle. Add, if required, salt and pepper. When the sauce is smooth and boiling, add the peas and mushrooms and simmer for another 3 to 5 minutes. Sprinkle with chopped parsley and serve with toast.

Pea and tomato pie
Skin 8 oz (225g) of tomatoes, slice, and cook in butter with a tablespoon of chopped onion until tender. Rub the pureé through a sieve. Place a layer of cooked cauliflower (about 2 cups) in a casserole, and add 2 cups of cooked peas, the tomato pureé, and ½ teaspoon of dried herbs mixed together. Season, top with mashed potato, pour over a beaten egg, and bake at 450° (gas mark 8) for 25 minutes or until golden-brown.

Pease pudding
Tie 8 oz (225g) of dried peas in butter muslin, allowing plenty of room for the peas to swell, and soak overnight in cold water. Next day, simmer until tender in salted water to which 1 teaspoon of sugar has been added. Rub through a sieve, season with salt and pepper, and add 1 oz of butter or margarine and a beaten egg. Tie tightly in a greased pudding cloth and steam or simmer for 30 minutes. Or place in a pie dish and bake for 30 minutes at 375° (gas mark 5).

Peppers

Also called pimentos, peppers are green, yellow or red according to ripeness. They are usually fried in butter. To prepare, split the peppers, cut away the stalks and remove the seeds. Slice thinly and fry gently for about 10 minutes. Season before serving.

Peppers can also be stuffed. With a sharp knife cut away the stalk ends and remove the seeds. Mix together 12 oz (350g) of sausage meat, 1 clove of chopped garlic, and 1 teaspoon of mixed herbs. Rub the peppers with olive oil or butter, place a rasher of bacon on each and bake at 375° (gas mark 5) for about 1 hour.

Potatoes

The Feast of Saints Peter and Paul (June 29th) used to have a big culinary significance for us when I was growing up. It was the day when, as a special treat, we dug the first stalk or two of the new potatoes.

They were watery, I remember, and not much bigger than marbles, but they tasted good after months of eating the old potatoes which, as we neared the bottom of the pit, had gone from bad to worse in quality.

I did not know then that there are a hundred ways of dressing up old potatoes to make them appetizing. Here are some of the nicest.

Note: In estimating quantities, 1 lb (450g) of old potatoes gives about 3 portions; 1 lb of new potatoes gives about 4 portions.

Baked potatoes
Wash and scrub 6 large even-sized potatoes. Dry and grease lightly with butter, margarine or dripping. Bake for 1 hour at 350° (gas mark 4). When the potatoes are half done, pull out the rack and quickly prick the skins once with a fork to permit the steam to escape, or cut two deep crosswise gashes in each potato. Return to the oven and finish baking.

Baked creamed potatoes
Dice 6 large cooked potatoes. Make ¾ pint (425ml) medium cream sauce and chop 3 hard-boiled eggs. Place the ingredients in 3 layers in a greased pie dish, and sprinkle the top with a mixture of 2 tablespoons of grated breadcrumbs and 2 tablespoons of grated cheese. Dot with butter and bake for 15 minutes at 375° (gas mark 5). Serve with halved grilled tomatoes and peas.

Baked stuffed potatoes
Bake 6 large potatoes. When done, cut a thin slice off the flat side, and with a spoon remove as much of the potato as possible without breaking the skin. Mix together 1 tablespoon of butter, 1 tablespoon (15ml) of cream, 1 tablespoon of chopped onion, 1 tablespoon of chopped parsley, 1 cup of chopped

cooked meat and ½ cup of gravy or stock to which has been added 1 teaspoon of Worcester sauce. Season with salt and paprika and fill the potato shells with the mixture, heaping the tops. Sprinkle each with grated cheese and bake at 400° (gas mark 6) until thoroughly hot and browned.

Baked potato chips
Peel medium-sized raw potatoes and cut them lengthwise into strips about ½ inch thick. Spread in a flat ovenproof dish. Pour over them about 3 tablespoons melted butter or margarine, and stir them around until well coated. Sprinkle with salt and pepper and bake in a hot oven at 450° (gas mark 8) for about 30 minutes. To get rid of excess fat, drain the chips on kitchen paper before serving.

Cheese potatoes
Bake 6 medium-sized potatoes. Cut a slice from the top of each, scoop out the inside, mash well, add 3 tablespoons of melted butter or margarine, 2 tablespoons (30ml) of hot milk, and 1 dessertspoon of chopped parsley. Season and beat until light and fluffy. Pile into shells, top with grated cheese and return to a hot oven until thoroughly reheated and the tops are lightly browned.

Chipped potatoes (French fries)
I am prepared to admit that no chips taste so good as those bought at the fish-and-chipper and eaten straight from the paper in which they are served. Still, we home cooks can prepare a passable imitation.

The important thing is to soak the chipped potatoes in cold salted water for at least one hour before frying. Or, if rushed for time, you may parboil them for about 2 minutes. In either case, the chips (cut in lengthwise strips about ¼ inch thick) should be well drained and dried. Bring a pan of deep fat to a temperature of 395° (hot enough to brown an inch cube of bread in 20 seconds). Put the chips into a chip basket and lower gently into the fat, and fry until golden-brown. To make sure the potatoes are done in the centre, test with a fork. Drain on paper, sprinkle with salt and serve very hot.

A good last minute time-saver is to partly cook the chips in advance. Use moderately hot fat and leave the chips in for a few minutes until they are tender but not brown. Drain and leave until required. Then heat the fat to boiling and plunge in the partly cooked chips. They will become crisp and brown in a few seconds. Drain well on paper, season and serve hot.

Coddled potatoes
This is Dublin's traditional Saturday night supper.

Choose small potatoes, about 1 lb (450g), and peel them thinly. Dice 4 oz (110g) of fat bacon, and sauté with 8 oz (225g) of onions until the onions are light brown. Add the potatoes, 1 tablespoon of chopped parsley, salt and pepper, and cover with 1 pint (570ml) of stock or water. Cover and simmer until the potatoes are cooked.

Colcannon

Did you ever eat colcannon when 'twas made with
*   yellow cream,*
And the kale and praties blended like the picture in a dream?
Did you ever take a forkful, and dip it in the lake
Of the heather-flavoured butter that your mother used
*   to make?*
Oh, you did; yes, you did. So did he and so did I,
And the more I think about it, sure the more I want to cry.
Ah, God be with the happy times, when troubles we had not,
And our mothers made colcannon in the little three-legged pot

To the old song's nostalgic questionnaire, I would add another query: Did you ever know the thrill of finding that lucky thruppenny-bit in your portion of our national Hallowe'en dish? And were you ever cruelly disappointed when what you hoped was a paper-wrapped coin turned out to be merely a lump of hard potato?

The prevention of such heartache is a simple matter. Here is a recipe for perfect colcannon. Put the cooked potatoes through a sieve or ricer. Beat in a good lump of butter or margarine and enough hot milk to make the mixture light and fluffy. Add to the potato mixture one-half its bulk of finely-chopped cooked kale and a tablespoonful of minced onion. Beat well and reheat thoroughly. And do not forget that all-important silver coin which, in view of the increased cost of sweet-eating, should be at least a sixpence.

(*Editor's note*, Alas, poor sixpence! 50p would seem to be in order today.)

Creamed potatoes
To 1½ lb (675g) of mashed cooked potatoes, add ¼ pint (150ml) of scalded milk in which 1½ oz (40g) of butter or margarine has been melted, and beat until creamy. Season and add 1 dessertspoon of finely chopped onion (optional) and 1 tablespoon of chopped parsley.

Croquette potatoes
Peel and mash 8 medium-sized potatoes. Add 2 tablespoons of melted butter or margarine, 3 tablespoons of grated cheese, 2 tablespoons (30ml) top of milk, 1 well-beaten egg, salt and pepper.

Form into croquettes with floured hands. Dilute 1 beaten egg with 1 tablespoon (15ml) of water. Roll the croquettes in the egg, then in the breadcrumbs. Place on a greased tin and bake at 375° (gas mark 5) for about 15 minutes. Or fry in deep fat.

Curried potatoes
Parboil 4 large potatoes in their jackets. peel while warm and cut into cubes. Brown a large chopped onion in fat in a deep pan, add the potatoes, spinkle with salt and 1 teaspoon of curry powder, then add ½ cup of stock, ½ cup of grated cheese and a squeeze of lemon juice. Cook for about 15 minutes, shaking now and then.

Duchesse potatoes
To 3 cups of riced or mashed potatoes, add 2 tablespoons of melted butter, 1½ beaten eggs and salt and pepper. Mix well and force through a tube or shape with two forks into little mounds on a greased baking sheet. Brush with the remainder of the beaten egg and cook in a very hot oven or under the grill until brown.

Grated fried potatoes

Scrub and grate coarsely (skin and all) 4 large potatoes, to which some grated onion may be added. Heat a little bacon fat in a frying-pan and spread out the grated potatoes. Cover and cook over a medium flame until the bottom is browned. Turn the pancake and brown the other side. Sprinkle with salt, pepper and parsley.

Hashed potatoes

Grate peeled raw potatoes, and for every 3 potatoes add a small chopped onion. Salt and pepper to taste. Melt butter or bacon fat in a large, heavy frying-pan and spread out the potatoes to a depth of about 1 inch. Cook (covered) over medium heat until the bottom is browned. Turn out the potato pancake carefully on to a large plate. Melt another knob of butter in the pan and slip the potatoes back on to it, taking care not to break the 'cake'. Cook until brown.

Lyonnaise potatoes

Melt 3 tablespoons of bacon fat in a frying-pan and add 3 cups of chopped boiled potatoes. Add a finely chopped small onion, $\frac{1}{4}$ cup of milk, salt and pepper, and cook slowly without stirring until well browned on the underside. Turn and brown the other side. Fold over like an omelette and serve at once.

Parslied potatoes

Scrape the skins of new potatoes and cook quickly in boiling salted water. Dry out over low heat, toss in melted butter and sprinkle with chopped parsley. Season with salt and pepper.

Potatoes aigrettes

Peel 1 lb (450g) of freshly boiled potatoes, rub through a sieve, and add 2 oz (50g) butter or margarine, and seasoning. Separate 3 eggs. Beat the yolks and whip the whites until stiff. Mix the yolks into the mashed potatoes and then fold in the whites. Heat deep fat until a thin blue smoke rises. Drop in the potato mixture in tablespoons and fry until golden brown.

Potatoes au gratin

Dice cold boiled potatoes and combine with cream sauce — about half as much sauce as there are potatoes. Put into a greased baking dish, cover with breadcrumbs and dot with butter. Bake at 400° (gas mark 6) until the crumbs are well browned.

Potato boats

Peel oval potatoes and hollow out the centres to make cup or boat shapes. Parboil for 10 minutes in boiling water, then drain and dry. Heat deep fat until hot enough to brown a cube in 20 seconds and fry the potatoes until golden-brown. Drain on kitchen paper and fill with any savoury mixture of vegetables and meat, to which the chopped potato centres have been added.

Potato cheese puffs

Beat 2 egg yolks. Add and beat until fluffy, 2 cups of cold or hot mashed potato, 3 tablespoons (45ml) of hot milk, and 2 tablespoons of grated cheese. Season with salt, paprika, and 1 teaspoon of finely chopped onion. Fold in 2 stiffly beaten egg whites and place the mixture in mounds on a greased tin. Brush the tops with melted butter and bake at 350° (gas mark 4) for 20 minutes.

Potatoes in bouillon

Peel 4 large potatoes and cut into quarters. Simmer with 4 minced scallions in 1½ cups of boiling stock until nearly tender. Drain. Make a roux with 1 tablespoon of butter or margarine, 1 tablespoon of flour and a little of the stock. Add the rest of the stock, bring to the boil, stirring well, and boil for 2 minutes. Return the potatoes to the pot and simmer them in the sauce until quite cooked. Season with salt, pepper and chopped parsley.

Potato pie

Peel and slice very thinly 6 medium-sized potatoes, and soak for 2 hours in cold water. Drain and dry them. Melt 2 table-spoons of butter or margarine in a heavy pan, add half of the potatoes, dot with butter and season with salt and pepper. Repeat with the remaining potatoes. Cook over a high heat until the potatoes are brown on the bottom — about ten minutes. Then cover and cook over a low flame until the potatoes are done — about 30 to 45 minutes. Dot the top with butter and brown under the grill. To serve, slice like pie.

Potato puffs

To 2 cups of hot mashed potatoes add 2 well-beaten eggs, 1 teaspoon of baking powder, salt and paprika. Beat well and drop by tablespoonfuls into boiling fat. Cook until brown and drain on absorbent paper.

Potato ribbons

Wash and peel large potatoes. Continue as though you were peeling, but rather more thickly. Put the ribbons into cold water and leave for 1 hour. Drain well and dry in a soft cloth, being careful not to break them. Fry in deep boiling fat until slightly crisp and golden brown. Drain well, keeping them very hot. Dust with salt and serve.

Potato scrapple

Mix equal quantities of cooked cabbage and mashed potato and season well. Add enough milk to make the mixture moist but not wet. Heat butter or margarine in a frying-pan until very hot. Turn the potato mixture on to the pan, spread evenly and fry until brown. Then turn it, cutting it roughly with the knife as it cooks — the idea being to make the finished result an appetizing collection of crisp brown pieces.

Scalloped potatoes

Peel and cut into very thick slices 1 lb (450g) of potatoes and 1 large onion. Place them in a greased baking dish in alternate layers, with the addition (optional) of a little diced bacon, raw or cooked. Season with salt, pepper and parsley. Add 1 cup of boiled milk and sprinkle with grated cheese. Cover and bake for about an hour at 350° (gas mark 4). Then remove the cover and continue cooking until the potatoes are crisp and golden.

Shoestring potatoes

These are usually served with game or with a mixed grill. The potatoes should be peeled and cut into very thin strips, like straws. Cook as for chips.

Soufflé potatoes

The recipe is slightly troublesome. But, since successful puffed potatoes are one of the hallmarks of the really accomplished cook, you may consider it worth while to master the method. And here's how:

Peel and slice 8 medium potatoes (the slices should not be more than ⅛ inch thick). Soak for 15 minutes in cold water, preferably ice water, and dry well in a towel. Prepare a pan of cooking fat and heat it moderately. The ideal temperature is 275°. Failing a kitchen thermometer, you may gauge the temperature fairly accurately with a cube of bread; if it takes 1 minute to brown, the heat is right. Fry the potatoes in the fat, 1 cupful at a time. Fry them slowly, allowing 5 minutes for this first frying, turning them once so as to ensure that they cook evenly. Spread them to drain on paper or a towel. When all the slices have been cooked, leave them to get thoroughly cold, preferably in the refrigerator (it is the sudden change of temperature from cold to boiling fat which causes the puffiness).

When the potatoes are required, heat the cooking fat until it is smoking hot (or until it will brown a cube of bread in 20 seconds). Plunge the partly fried potato slices, about 1 cupful at a time, into the boiling fat. They should puff immediately. Remove from the fat and spread to drain on paper. If you feel they are not sufficiently crisp, return them to the boiling fat for another minute or two. Sprinkle lightly with salt, and serve at once.

Stewed potatoes

These are very good with cold meat. Dice a fat rasher of bacon and fry until crisp. Sauté until lightly browned a medium-sized chopped onion and 6 potatoes peeled and cut into ½ inch cubes; then add a large cup of boiling stock or water, a bay leaf, salt and pepper. Cover and simmer for about 10 minutes or until the potatoes are tender but not mushy. Drain and serve sprinkled with parsley.

Salsify

Salsify is boiled in salted water until tender, then drained and served with melted butter or in a cream sauce.

Cooked salsify can also be dipped in batter and fried in deep fat until golden-brown. Drain well before serving.

Sea kale

One of the best and most delicate of all vegetables.

Cut away the dark woody base, and either slice in 3 inch pieces or tie in bundles of 5 to 6 and cook (covered) in very little salted water until it is tender but firm. Serve with melted butter or Hollandaise sauce.

Spinach

There is a classic *New Yorker* cartoon which shows an anxious mother coaxing her fractious child to absorb his vitamins. The caption runs:

'But it's broccoli, dear.'

'I say it's spinach, and I say the heck with it!'

Try these ways of cooking spinach (and the other less usual vegetables). They are guaranteed to make even the most difficult children eat without acrimony.

Buttered spinach

Remember that spinach reduces considerably in the cooking, and allow at least 8 oz (225g) of uncooked spinach per person. Pick the leaves from the stalks and wash it quickly in several waters to free it from sand and grit. Put the washed spinach into a saucepan containing absolutely no water. Cover and simmer gently until the juice begins to run. Now add a little salt, increase the heat and cook rapidly until the spinach is tender.

Perfectly cooked spinach should not need draining (removing the lid during the last few minutes of cooking will help to drive off surplus moisture). If any moisture does remain, drain it off, then cut up the spinach finely with 2 sharp knives. Sauté 1 tablespoon of finely chopped onion in 1 tablespoon of butter or bacon fat. Mix this into the spinach, together with a squeeze of lemon juice and salt and pepper to taste.

Creamed spinach
To spinach cooked as in preceding recipe add 1 cup of medium cream sauce. Mix well, and serve it garnished with slices of hard-boiled egg.

Spinach pancakes
On small pancakes place 1 tablespoon of creamed spinach and 1 dessertspoon of sliced sautéed mushrooms. Roll up the pancakes, place on a fireproof dish, sprinkle with grated cheese and place under the grill until the cheese is melted.

Spinach timbales
Cook 1½–2 lb (675–900g) of fresh spinach until tender but still crisp. Drain and chop finely. Add 3 slightly beaten eggs, ½ pint (275ml), 1 teaspoon of grated onion, salt and pepper, and pour into greased custard cups (¾ full). Set in a pan of hot water and bake for 25 to 30 minutes, or until firm, at 375° (gas mark 5).

Place tomato slices on rounds of toast and place under the grill for a few minutes. Top with the spinach timbales and some egg sauce. Sprinkle with parsley.

Tomatoes

Baked tomatoes
Place whole or halved tomatoes in a shallow greased baking tin. Sprinkle with equal quantities of minced chives and breadcrumbs, and season with salt and pepper. Dot with butter or margarine, and bake for 20 to 30 minutes at 350° (gas mark 4).

Broiled tomatoes
If the tomatoes are very large, cut into thick slices; otherwise cut them in half. Dot with butter, sprinkle with some herbs, pepper and salt. Broil for about 5 minutes under a low heat. They should not be cooked longer than it will take to heat them thoroughly.

Fried tomatoes

Fry thick slices of tomato in butter or other fat over a low heat until crisped on both sides, and remove to a hot plate. Some cream added to the pan and simmered until brown over low heat makes a nice sauce to serve with the tomatoes. Season with salt and pepper.

Stewed tomatoes

Peel and quarter 1 lb (450g) of tomatoes. Sauté 1 teaspoon of chopped onion in 2 oz (50g) of butter or margarine, add a teaspoon of sugar, salt and pepper, cover and simmer until tender. Just before serving, add 1 cup of diced fried bread.

Stuffed tomatoes (baked)

Cut large hollows in unpeeled tomatoes. Salt, and invert to drain for 20 minutes, then fill with any desired combination of cooked food. Cover the tops with breadcrumbs, dot with butter and sprinkle with grated cheese. Place the tomato cases in a dish with barely enough water to keep them from burning, and bake at 350° (gas mark 4) for 10 to 15 minutes until they are cooked (but not long enough to become so soft that they lose their shape).

Filled tomatoes are good on toast, or with grills or roasts.

Stuffed tomatoes (uncooked)

Some people like to fill tomato cases with cold food and serve with salads.

To prepare for filling: Cut a slice from the tomato and hollow it (or, if you want small portions, use halved tomatoes). Invert and drain for 20 minutes. Any of the following fillings can be used:

Aspic filling: Add to $1\frac{1}{2}$ cups of aspic, 1 cup of mixed vegetables or a mixture of flaked fish and vegetables, or diced cooked meat. When the aspic is about to set, fill the tomato cases. When firm, garnish with parsley. Serve with mayonnaise on a bed of lettuce.

Egg and anchovies: Combine 2 chopped hard-boiled eggs, 1 teaspoon of anchovy paste, 1 teaspoon of grated onion, and 1 teaspoon of chopped parsley. Season with salt and pepper, and bind with mayonnaise or sour cream.

Egg and ham filling: Combine 2 chopped hard-boiled eggs, 1 cup of minced ham, a couple of chopped olives and a tablespoon of chopped pickles. Bind with sour cream or mayonnaise.

Vegetable filling: Combine cooked peas, cooked diced potatoes, chopped raw onion and diced tomato. Season and bind with salad dressing.

Scalloped tomatoes
Peel 1½ lb (675g) of tomatoes, slice thinly, and spread a layer in the bottom of a greased casserole. Combine 2 cups of bread-crumbs with 1 medium chopped onion, 3 tablespoons of melted butter, ½ teaspoon of sugar, and season with salt and pepper. Cover the tomatoes with a layer of the mixture, add another layer of tomatoes, then more mixture, until it is all used up; the top layer should be of tomatoes. Top with 4 table-spoons of grated cheese and bake for 25 minutes at 375° (gas mark 5).

Tomato rarebit
Shell and slice 4 hard-boiled eggs. Sauté 2 tablespoons of chopped onion in 2 tablespoons of butter or margarine until soft. Add the contents of a medium-sized tin of tomato soup and, when the ingredients are hot, reduce the heat and stir in 4 oz (110g) of grated cheese. When the cheese is melted, pour a little of the sauce over a beaten egg, mix well and add to the sauce. Stir in 1 teaspoon of Worcester sauce, and season with salt and pepper. Stir over very low heat until the sauce thickens slightly, but on no account should it boil.

Arrange the sliced eggs on a large dish, surround with mashed potatoes and top with the sauce.

Tomato pie
Skin and halve some large tomatoes. Hollow out the centres, sprinkle with salt and pepper, and break a raw egg into each.

Make a sauce as follows: Sauté 1 tablespoon of chopped onion and 1 tablespoon of chopped celery in 2 oz (50g) of butter or margarine until soft. Blend 1½ tablespoons of flour into the mixture and stir until light brown. Mash up the tomato centres, add to ¾ pint (425ml) of stock or water and add to the onion mixture. Cook, stirring constantly, for 3 minutes. Season with salt, pepper and ½ teaspoon of sugar.

Line a pie dish with mashed potato, and place the tomato shells and eggs in the dish. Pour the sauce over, sprinkle thickly with breadcrumbs and bake for 20 minutes at 375° (gas mark 5).

Note: To skin tomatoes, simply plunge into very hot water for about 5 minutes.

Turnips

Turnips should be served as a vegetable only when very young.

Swede turnips

Peel, slice or cube, and cook in boiling salted water until tender. Mash or leave whole. Season and dress with melted butter or bacon fat.

White turnips

Peel and cube turnips and cook until tender in boiling salted water. Serve with parsley sauce.

Vegetables — general

Vegetable garnishes

To make plain buttered vegetables more attractive, serve them with one of these garnishes: Minced parsley, minced green onion tops or chives, sieved hard-cooked egg yolks, grated cheese (place dish under grill and broil until cheese is melted), crisp fried bacon (crumbled), buttered crumbs.

Vegetable rissoles

Roll shortcrust pastry thinly and cut into 3-inch squares. Put a spoonful of vegetable purée or vegetable croquette mixture on each square. Brush the edges with beaten egg, fold over and press together with a fork. These may be fried in deep fat or cooked in the oven. If baked, brush with beaten egg before giving them 15 minutes at 450° (gas mark 8). Serve with cheese sauce or tomato sauce.

Vegetable hot-pot

Prepare and slice raw potatoes, celery, carrots and onions, allowing for each person 2 potatoes and a half cup each of celery, carrot and onion. Place layers of the vegetables in a pie dish, seasoning each layer well with salt and pepper, finishing with a layer of potatoes. Add sufficient boiling water or stock to just cover the vegetables. Cover and simmer in a moderate oven for 1 hour or until the vegetables are tender. Dot the top with butter and serve very hot.

Salads

Preparing the ingredients: Salad greens may consist of lettuce, endive, chicory, green cabbage leaves, dandelion leaves or water cress. They should be crisp, cold, fresh and dry. Wash the leaves separately, pat gently in a clean cloth until dry, wrap loosely in a porous damp cloth and keep until required in a cold place or – preferably – in a covered dish in the refrigerator.

Other ingredients should be cut in distinct, shapely pieces; do not mash or allow them to become soft or mushy. Attractive pieces may be made by cutting slices, wedges, dice, circles, julienne strips, etc. Vegetables should be thoroughly drained before combining; this prevents wateriness which is always undesirable in a salad. Cooked vegetables, meat, chicken or cooked potatoes are improved by being marinated in French dressing for at least one hour before serving.

Combining the salad: Salads should never be stirred. The ingredients should be tossed together lightly, taking care to blend the dressing with each and every piece, but at the same time being careful not to mash or crush them. This painstaking blending of ingredients is what the French call 'fatiguing' the salad.

Serving: Correct arrangement on the salad plate or in the bowl is all important to the attractiveness of the salad. The greens should be crisp and perky. They should stand up around the salad mixture rather than lie flat. The leaves should not extend out over the margin of the plate. Salads are often masked or spread smoothly with mayonnaise. This is usually done as a background for garnishing.

Garnishes: Choose simple fresh garnishes, not too elaborate, and of appropriate colour and flavour.

Some suggestions: Radish 'roses' or 'tulips', celery curls, onion rings, pickle fans, slices or sections of hard-boiled eggs, stuffed olives, chopped chives, ribbons of chicory; sprigs of water-cress or parsley. Or, use diamonds, stars or match-sticks of carrots or slices of tomato.

If the salad is to be topped with mayonnaise, add the topping just before serving in order to preserve a crisp freshness.

Pea and tomato salad

Cut the top off large ripe tomatoes and scoop out the centres. Make a salad dressing with equal quantities of mayonnaise and fresh or sour cream. Season this well and use to moisten cooked green peas, or a mixture of peas and diced cooked potatoes. Fill the tomato cases with this mixture and serve on lettuce leaves that have been dressed with seasoned oil and vinegar.

Picnic salad

Mix equal quantities of cubed cucumbers, tomatoes, onions and cold boiled potatoes. Marinate lightly in French dressing, then bind with mayonnaise.

Potato salad

Peel 1 lb (450g) of freshly boiled potatoes. Dice and toss gently in 2 tablespoons of French dressing. When cold, mix in 2 tablespoons of mayonnaise, 2 tablespoons of chopped spring onions and 1 dessertspoon of chopped parsley.

For best results the potatoes should be marinated while hot in French dressing.

Russian salad

Combine the following cooked vegetables, diced small: 2 medium potatoes, 1 large carrot, 1 cup of peas. ½ cup of French beans, 1 cup of cauliflower sprigs, and 1 tomato. Sprinkle the vegetables with salt and pepper to taste and bind with barely as much mayonnaise as will adhere.

Winter salads

How did we get into the bad habit of serving salads only in spring and summer? It is irrational, to say the least, that we should treat ourselves to health-giving greens and uncooked vegetables only during those months when, thanks to the sunshine, we need them least.

Winter is the time when tired systems can do with the purifying effect of salads and when tired complexions will benefit most from their magic juices. Once we rid ourselves of the illusion that a salad must be based on lettuce, we can see that the winter months offer plenty of crisp inviting salad ingredients. For greens, use tender shredded cabbage hearts and Brussels sprouts; for zest, onion rings; for crunchiness, celery and carrots; for colour, sliced beetroot and tomato. For added heartiness, build your salad around a mound of diced cooked potato coated with creamy mayonnaise. And don't forget that there is health in parsley, so use a liberal sprinkling on every salad you serve.

Egg salad

With a fork crush 8 hard-boiled eggs and stir in 3 tablespoons of butter, ½ teaspoon of dry mustard, 3 tablespoons (45ml) of lemon juice, and 1 tablespoon (15ml) of Worcester sauce. Now add 3 tablespoons of mayonnaise (45ml) and mix well. Mould with 2 tablespoons.

For each serving, place greens tossed with French dressing on a plate. Place a thick slice of tomato in the centre, and on each tomato slice place a mound of the egg mixture. Sprinkle with chopped olives.

French bean salad (1)

Mix together well 3 tablespoons (45ml) of olive oil, 1 tablespoon (15ml) of lemon juice, 1 tablespoon of chopped green pepper, and 1 tablespoon of minced onion. Season. Toss 8 oz (225g) of cooked French beans in this dressing and serve with crisp lettuce and tomato slices.

French bean salad (2)

Toss 8 oz (225g) of French beans in mayonnaise and arrange in a salad bowl. Place a ring of sliced ripe tomatoes around the beans. Cut two hard-boiled eggs into slices. Rub the yolks through a sieve and mix with an equal amount of mayonnaise. Place a ring of egg white on each slice of tomato and fill with the mayonnaise mixture.

Meat salad
Dice any cooked meat, or flaked, firm cooked fish. Add about half as much cooked diced potato, a chopped onion and a sprinkling of chopped parsley. Bind with mayonnaise or season well with French dressing. Serve on dressed lettuce or other greens.

Jellied salads
The success of these dishes depends on the aspic or savoury jelly. It should be well flavoured and should set firmly. It is possible to buy ready prepared aspic, but this is hardly worthwhile as it may be made at home quite easily.

Basic recipe: Allow 1 oz (25g) of sheet or powdered gelatine to 1 pint of well-seasoned stock. Add a little of the cold stock to the gelatine and leave for 5 minutes. Then add the remainder of the stock, hot but not boiling, and stir until the gelatine is completely dissolved. When cold and about to set, combine the aspic with 1½ cups of solid ingredients.

Ingredients suitable for jellied salads are a choice or combination of any of the following: Cooked diced meat, cooked flaked fish, hard-boiled eggs, shredded cabbage, quartered tomatoes, diced celery or cucumbers, sliced green peppers, cooked cauliflower sprigs, pickles, sliced or cubed cooked beetroot, cooked or raw carrots, chopped parsley, chives or other herbs.

Celery salt, lemon juice and paprika are frequently used to pep up jellied salads.

Chicken or fish mousse
Soak 1 oz (25g) of gelatine in 2 tablespoons of cold water. Add ½ cup of hot stock or water and stir until dissolved. When cold, add 1 cup of mayonnaise, 1 tablespoon (15ml) of lemon juice, 1 tablespoon of grated onion, salt and paprika to taste.

When the mixture begins to set, fold in ½ cup of stiffly whipped cream. Fold into the gelatine mixture 2 cups of finely flaked fish or finely chopped cooked chicken, and place in a wetted mould. When set, unmould and serve with lettuce.

Jellied salmon salad
Prepare aspic according to the basic recipe. When cold and about to set, add ¼ cup of diced cucumber and 1 cup of flaked cooked salmon or tuna fish and 1 chopped hard-boiled egg. Unmould when set and decorate with alternating slices of tomato and cucumber.

Salad ring
A jellied salad moulded in a ring, with the centre piled with diced meat or vegetables bound with mayonnaise, is a very attractive dish. A wetted angel cake tin is the ideal mould. Failing one of these ring tins, you can improvise a mould by standing a wetted jam jar in any round bowl or tin. Pour the aspic around the jam jar. To unmould the jelly, pour a little hot water into the jam jar and remove it immediately. Then turn the aspic on to a dish in the usual way and fill the centre with any desired mixture.

Tomato aspic
Combine 1 lb (450g) of sliced tomatoes, 1 tablespoon (15ml) of lemon juice, 1½ teaspoons of sugar, a bay leaf, salt and pepper. Add sufficient water to keep the tomatoes from burning and simmer for 15 minutes. Strain and add sufficient hot water to make almost 1 pint (570ml) of liquid. Add 1 oz (25g) of gelatine which has been soaked in a little cold water, and stir well.

When the aspic is about to set, add 1 cup of cooked chopped meat or flaked fish and ½ cup of cooked peas. When firm, unmould the salad on to a bed of lettuce leaves and decorate with mayonnaise or with seasoned whipped cream.

Meat

On a bleak day, even to think of Statia Dunne's stew brings comfort. That was a monarch among stews. It won Statia many a compliment. It won her a husband — and at an age when she had almost given up hope of ever having a man of her own to cook for.

Statia was not the type to catch a man's eye. She had pale hair and skin, and she was as small and shy as a wren. Given a little leisure, she might have done something with herself, but caring for her bed-ridden father and for her three bachelor brothers left her with barely enough time to bless herself.

She was nearing forty when Dr. Crowley came to our place. He was at the age when a man who is not married begins to show the need of a woman who'll see that his clothes are pressed and his collars properly laundered, and who'll make sure that he eats good regular meals. Poor Dr. Crowley looked lost and neglected.

He was called out to old Mr. Dunne during that spell of cold stormy weather we had five — or was it six? — years ago.

The house was filled with the smell of Statia's stew. It was a tantalizing smell, made up of twenty different fragrances. As Dr. Crowley was drawing on his gloves, he nodded in the direction of the kitchen. 'That's a grand smell,' he said shyly.

Statia said afterwards that he looked like a child putting in for a treat. The lost look of him, coupled with the way the sleet was pelting the windows, made her say quickly, 'Wouldn't you stay and have a bit? I was just putting it on the table.'

Dr. Crowley found the look of the stew even more tantalizing than the smell. Statia believed in serving a good dish in the style it deserved. Around the edge of a big platter, she built a rampart of fluffy mashed potato. That was given a quick brown-up in the oven, after which she bedewed it with parsley, chopped powder-fine. The stew was turned into this gold-and-jade ring. Brown of tender meat cubes mingled with the white of celery and turnip, the bright green of peas and the yellow and orange of carrots, the whole soused in gravy as dark and as rich as a maharajah.

That gravy was the making of Statia's stew. Years of practice had gone to finding out the exact amount of mustard that should be added for tanginess, of sugar for the faint underlying sweetness and of vinegar for a teasing sharpness. It had a leaf of this herb, a sprig of that. And it was full of the goodness of the meat and vegetable juices that had run into it during the slow careful cooking.

Dr. Crowley cleared his plate. As he stood up to go, Statia could not help thinking that if only his clothes were pressed once in a while, he could look as prosperous and as comfortable as any doctor in Ireland.

'Do you know,' he said, 'I haven't eaten a meal like that since my mother died, God rest her.'

'We have stew every Saturday during the cold weather,' Statia told him. 'You're welcome any time you're passing.'

In the way one thing leads to another, Dr. Crowley got acquainted with Statia's stuffed steak, her coddled rabbit and her baked liver loaf served with scalloped potatoes. Before he was half way through her culinary repertoire, they were engaged.

She took old Mr. Dunne to live with them when they got married. And her eldest brother Paddy, who had been keeping company with Leesha Flood for 16 years, married the girl and brought her home to take Statia's place. So that she might do this adequately, Statia brought a twopenny copybook and wrote out the best of her recipes for her.

Incidentally, Statia's trick of serving the stew in a ring of toasted mashed potato was one she often employed when she wanted to dress up creamed vegetables or fish, or left-over meat heated in gravy.

Meat

Suit the cooking to the cut is the first rule in successful meat cooking. The tender fine-grained cuts may be grilled, fried or roasted. Tough cuts need slow cooking in moist heat.

There are few cuts which will not benefit in texture and flavour from being marinated before cooking. A marinade is a mixture of cider, wine, vinegar and/or oil, with or without herbs. The meat should be placed in a deep dish, the marinade poured over it and then left — preferably in the refrigerator — to soak for a few hours before cooking. Turn occasionally.

Cider marinade: Combine ¾ pint (425ml) of cider, 2 small chopped onions, ¼ teaspoon each of ginger and cinnamon, 2 tablespoons of sugar and 3 cloves.

French marinade: Combine ½ pint (275ml) of French dressing (unsalted) with 2 teaspoons of dried herbs or 2 tablespoons of fresh herbs (parsley, chives, mint, thyme), and 1 teaspoon of peppercorns.

Wine marinade: Combine ½ pint (275ml) of acid white or red wine with ½ cup of salad oil, 1 tablespoon each of chopped parsley and grated onion, and bay leaf.

After use, the marinade may be kept in the refrigerator or a cold place for future use, or it may be strained, added to the stock in which the meat is cooked and used to make a delicious gravy.

Note: When cooking stuffed meat or meat that is boned and rolled, allow an extra 5 minutes per lb.

Beef

In season all the year round, beef should be hung for as long as possible. The fat should be creamy-white and the lean should be bright red. Choose meat that is moderately fat; very lean meat means poor quality.

Boiled beef

Cuts: brisket (corned or fresh), aitchbone, silverside (salt or fresh)

Cooking: Boiling time required for tenderness will depend on the age and quality of the beef. Good beef should not take more than 30 minutes per lb.

Wipe meat with a damp cloth (wash if necessary), trim and tie in shape, or skewer. Put it into a saucepan with or without vegetables and added enough boiling water to cover. Add salt (2 teaspoons for 4 to 6 lbs of meat), a sprinkling of pepper, and bring to the boil. Skim. Cover closely, reduce heat and simmer until the meat is tender.

Braised beef
Cuts: Backribs, flank (thick or thin), round steak.
Cooking: Braising is ideal for tenderizing cheaper cuts of meat. Brown the meat over moderate heat, then place with a little liquid (with or without vegetables) in a covered casserole. Cook very slowly at 300°–350° (gas mark 2 to 3).

Braised beef with vegetables	2 rashers streaky bacon 2 lb lean beef (900g) 1 pint stock or water (570g) 1 cup each of diced carrots and onions 6 halved potatoes 1 tablespoon flour Salt and pepper

Dice and fry the rashers over a low heat until crisp. Cut the beef into cubes and sear quickly on all sides in the fat. Place in a casserole, rinse out the pan with boiling stock or water and pour it over the meat. Cover and bake in a slow oven at 300° (gas mark 2) for about 3½ hours. For the last ½ hour add the carrots, onions and potatoes. When cooked, remove the meat and vegetables, and thicken the gravy with *beurre manié* and season.

Frying
Cuts: Steak — sirloin, fillet, rump or point. Use only meat that has been well hung and beat it before cooking. For juiciness and tenderness the steak should be at least 1 inch thick.
Cooking: Steak improves in flavour and tenderness if left to marinate in French dressing or other marinade for an hour before cooking.

Trim excess fat from a beefsteak (rump, sirloin or fillet) 2 inches thick, and rub with a clove of garlic. Score the steak every 2 inches around the edge to keep it from curling. Sear the steak on both sides in a dry pan over a strong heat. When the steak is browned on both sides, reduce the heat and cook, turning twice, until it reaches the desired stage of doneness (8 to 10 minutes). Season.

A small or thin steak ($\frac{1}{4}$ to $\frac{1}{2}$ inch thick) is called a minute steak and requires only about 4 to 5 minutes cooking.

Do not overcook steak. The perfect steak is crisp and brown on the outside and rare to medium inside.

Steak is served with *maitre d'hotel* butter, gravy, or a sauce such as Bearnaise or wine sauce.

Grilling

Cuts: As for frying.

Cooking: Preheat the grill. The steak should be about 2 inches from the heat. For a minute steak, allow 1 minute for each side; for a 1 inch steak allow 5 minutes for the first side and 3 minutes for the second side.

Pot roasting

Cuts: Chuck or round steak, topside, silverside.

Cooking: Pot roasting is ideal for cheaper cuts of meat. The essential piece of equipment is a heavy saucepan with a tight fitting lid. The meat is seared, then cooked very slowly in a small quantity of stock or cider, with or without vegetables. The steam from the liquid inside the pot keeps the meat deliciously tender.

Beef pot roast

3 lb round steak (1350g)
2 tablespoon flour
2 tablespoons beef dripping
2 tablespoons chopped onions
1 pint stock (570ml)
1 teaspoon dried herbs
Salt and pepper

Rub the meat with garlic and dredge with the flour. Heat the dripping in a heavy saucepan and sauté the onions lightly.

Remove the onions and sear the meat quickly on all sides until it is dark brown. Pour the stock over it — there should be about ½ inch of liquid in the saucepan. Reduce the heat and cover closely. Bring slowly to simmering point — the meat must not boil — and simmer slowly until tender (about 3 hours). Add the onions 30 minutes before the meat is done, and season.

Beef pot roast (in cider)
Use the same ingredients as for Beef Pot Roast. Soak the meat for 1½ hours in 1 pint of cider marinade. Pat dry, dredge with seasoned flour and proceed as for Beef Pot Roast, using the strained marinade instead of stock.

Beef pot roast (Italian)

2 lb chuck beef (900g)
3 tablespoons olive oil (45ml)
1 lb sliced tomatoes (450g)
½ clove garlic
½ bay leaf, 1 clove
Salt and pepper

Roll and tie the meat and sear in hot olive oil. Add the tomatoes, garlic, bay leaf, clove, and season. Cover tightly and simmer for 3 hours until tender. Remove the garlic, clove and bay leaf. Thicken gravy, if necessary, by stirring in *beurre manié*, simmer for a few minutes, then strain.

Roasting
Cuts: Aitchbone, foreribs, sirloin, top rib (thick or thin), top rump, topside (best cut), wing rib, whole fillet or undercut.
Cooking: Allow 15 minutes to the lb, and 15 minutes over. Start at 475° (gas mark 9), and after 15 minutes reduce to 350° (gas mark 4). Baste every 15 minutes.

Roast beef should be served underdone, pink in the centre. It is served with gravy or Bearnaise sauce.

Stewing
Strictly speaking, stewing refers to cooking on the top of the stove, casseroling to cooking in the oven. For ease of reference

(as we tend to think of them both in the same way) I have put both sets of recipes under this one heading.

Cuts: Chuck steak, round steak, topside.

There are three very good reasons for serving stew frequently.

1. It's easy: Once the meat is browned and the liquid added, stew will cook without attention. And this one-dish meal saves washing up.

2. It's economical: Less expensive cuts may be used, as the long slow simmering will make them tender.

3. It's tasty: The savoury combination of tender meat and vegetables cooked in their own juices, pepped up with clever seasoning, makes stew one of the tastiest meals possible.

Now three rules for perfect stews:

1. Trim excess fat from the meat to avoid greasiness and make sure that the liquid never goes higher than simmering point.

2. Add vegetables at the right moment; they must not be overcooked.

3. Have the gravy satin smooth and full of flavour. Be enterprizing with seasoning — try adding a dash of celery salt, a scrap of garlic, a few tablespoons of cider or wine, a sprinkling of herbs.

Beef stew (old fashioned)

2½ lb lean chuck steak (1125g)
2 tablespoons flour
Salt, pepper, and paprika
3 tablespoons beef dripping
Stock or water
12 small chopped onions
6 small carrots
8 halved potatoes
Chopped parsley

Cut the meat into 2-inch cubes. Mix the flour with the seasonings and dredge the meat with it. Brown quickly in the dripping, add the onion and cook for a few minutes longer. Transfer to a saucepan and add barely enough hot stock or water to cover the meat. Cover and simmer for 2 hours or until almost tender. Add the onions, carrots and potatoes and continue cooking for another 35 minutes or until the vegetables are done. Serve in a deep dish and sprinkle finely chopped parsley on top.

Beef stew Gaston

8 oz streaky bacon (225g)
2 lb lean beef (900g)
1 tablespoon flour
Salt and pepper
2 pints stock (1140ml)
1 clove garlic
1 large chopped onion
8 oz sliced tomatoes (225g)
12 peppercorns
3 cloves
2 tablespoons chopped parsley
$\frac{1}{2}$ bay leaf
1 glass sherry or cider
6 peeled quartered potatoes
2 sliced carrots
2 stalks chopped celery

Dice the bacon and fry over a slow heat. Cut the beef into pieces and brown quickly in the bacon fat. Sprinkle with seasoned flour. In a heavy saucepan, combine and cook until boiling $\frac{1}{2}$ pint (275ml) of stock, garlic, onion, tomatoes, peppercorns, cloves, parsley and bay leaf. Add the meat together with the rest of the stock, cover and simmer for about $3\frac{1}{2}$ hours. Add the sherry or cider and cook for about $\frac{1}{2}$ hour. Cook separately until nearly tender the potatoes, carrots and celery and add to the stew for the last 15 minutes of cooking.

Beef and kidney casserole

$1\frac{1}{2}$ lb round steak (675g)
3 lamb kidneys
1 medium chopped onion
2 tablespoons flour
Salt and pepper
2 tablespoons beef dripping
1 pint stock or water (570ml)

1 tablespoon Worcester sauce
1 large sliced carrot
6 halved potatoes

Cut the steak into fingers. Split the kidneys, remove the tubes and soak in cold salted water for ½ hour, then cut into small pieces. Lightly brown the onion in the dripping. Season the flour, coat the steak and kidney and brown well. Arrange the meat, onion and carrot in layers in a large casserole and add the stock and sauce. Cover and cook at 350° (gas mark 4) for 1½ hours, then add the potatoes. Cover and continue cooking for another hour.

Beef and kidney hotpot

8 oz beef kidney (225g)
1½ lb round steak (675g)
Salt and pepper
6 sliced potatoes
2 sliced onions
2 sliced carrots
2 sticks sliced celery
1 tablespoon chopped parsley
Stock or water

Slice and trim the kidney. Trim the beef and cut into 2 inch pieces. Season the flour and coat with meat with it. Place a layer of potatoes at the bottom of the casserole, then a layer of onions, carrot, celery and meat. Sprinkle with parsley, season lightly, and repeat the layering until all the ingredients have been used up. The top layer must be of potatoes.

Add sufficient stock or water almost to cover. Cover and simmer at 350° (gas mark 4) for about 2½ hours. During the last 30 minutes of cooking, remove the lid, baste the potato topping lightly with bacon fat or butter and finish cooking, uncovered, until the potatoes are brown. Serve in the casserole.

Beef and kidney stew

2 tablespoons pearl barley
2 pints water (1140ml)
8 oz beef kidney (225g)
1 lb rump steak (450g)

2 tablespoons flour
Salt and pepper
2½ tablespoons dripping or bacon fat
2 large sliced onions
1 bay leaf
4 sliced carrots
1 chopped green pepper

Soak the barley overnight in the water. Remove the skin from the kidneys, remove membranes and fat, and cut into 1-inch pieces. Trim the steak and cut into 2-inch fingers. Season the flour with salt and pepper, and coat the meat with it. Brown in the fat, then add the onions and continue cooking for 5 minutes. Add the barley, water and bay leaf, cover and simmer for 1½ hours at 350° (gas mark 4). Add the carrots and pepper and simmer for another 30 minutes.

Beef olives

1½ lb lean beef (675g)
1 cup breadcrumbs
1 dessertspoon chopped onion
¼ tablespoon sage
1 egg
1 small tin unsweetened milk
2 tablespoons flour
Salt and pepper
2 tablespoons fat

Cut the meat into strips about 5 inch x 3 inch, and pound to ¼ inch thick. Make a stuffing with the breadcrumbs, onion, sage and egg, and 2 tablespoons of the milk. Spread on each slice of meat. Roll tightly and tie or skewer. Season 1 tablespoon of flour, dredge the meat with it and sear quickly in hot fat. Put the olives into a casserole. Pour off all but 1 tablespoon of fat in the pan and brown 1 tablespoon of flour in it. Add the remainder of the milk, mixed with stock or water to bring it to ¾ pint (425ml), and bring to the boil stirring constantly. Pour over the olives, cover and cook for 1¼ hours at 375° (gas mark 5).

Serve with tomato sauce.

Casserole
bonne femme

2 lb beef (900g)
1 tablespoon dripping
Bouquet garni
2 sliced onions
2 sliced carrots
½ head sliced celery
1 tablespoon flour
¼ pint cider (150ml)
¼ pint stock (150ml)
1 tablespoon tomato catsup
Salt and pepper

Trim the meat and cut into 2-inch cubes. Brown quickly in the fat, and place in a casserole with the bouquet garni, onions, carrots, celery and parsley. Add to the fat in the pan, the flour, cider, stock and tomato catsup. Season, boil up and add to the casserole. Cover and cook at 325° (gas mark 3) for about 2½ hours. Remove the meat to a dish, sieve the vegetables and gravy and pour the purée over the meat. Serve with a border of boiled rice, macaroni or mashed potatoes.

Goulash

2 oz dripping (50g)
2 large chopped onions
2 lb beef or veal (900g)
1 tablespoon flour
¾ pint stock (425ml)
½ pint red wine or cider (275ml)
Salt and paprika
2 tablespoons tomato catsup

Melt the fat in a heavy frying-pan and cook the onions until lightly browned. Cut the meat into small cubes and brown on all sides. Put the meat and onions into a casserole. Brown the flour in the fat remaining in the pan, add the stock, cider or wine and seasonings. Bring to the boil, stirring well, and then pour into the casserole. Cover and cook for 2½ hours at 325° (gas mark 3).

Oxtail stew

4 lb oxtail (1800g)
2 tablespoons fat
1 large chopped onion

2 pints stock or water (1140ml)
Salt, pepper, bay leaf
1 tablespoons flour
1 tablespoon chopped chives

Cut up the oxtail and brown in the fat. Add the onion. Put the oxtail into a casserole, add the water and seasonings. Cover and cook slowly for 2 hours or until the meat almost falls from the bones. Skim off the fat. Thicken the liquid with *beurre manié*, bring to the boil and simmer for about 5 minutes.

Fill the centre of a large meat platter with a mound of mashed potato, boiled rice or macaroni. Surround with the oxtail and gravy, sprinkle with chives and serve very hot.

Statia Dunne's stew

2 lb round steak (900g)
1½ tablespoons flour
Salt and pepper
¼ teaspoon dry mustard
2 tablespoons bacon fat
1 pint water (570ml)
1 teaspoon yeast extract
1 teaspoon vinegar
1 teaspoon sugar
Bouquet garni
4 stalks chopped celery
2 medium chopped onions
3 medium diced carrots
1 diced white turnip
2 sliced tomatoes
1 dessertspoon chopped parsley

Trim the meat and cut into 1-inch cubes. Season the flour with salt, pepper and mustard. Roll the meat in the flour, brown quickly in the fat, and put into a stewpan. Blend the remainder of the flour with the fat in the pan, stir in the water, yeast extract, vinegar and sugar, and bring to the boil. Pour over the meat, add the bouquet garni and simmer for 1½ hours at 325° (gas mark 3). Add the vegetables and continue simmering until they are tender. Remove the bouquet garni and serve the stew in a browned border of mashed potatoes sprinkled with parsley.

Corned beef

If the beef is very salty, steep overnight. Next day, place in a stewpan with enough cold water to cover. Bring slowly to the boil, skim thoroughly, cover closely and simmer until tender. Corned beef that is to be eaten cold is best cooled in the water in which it was cooked.

Moulded corned beef

1 oz gelatine (25g)
½ cup cold water
1 pint stock (570ml)
¼ teaspoon Worcester sauce
Salt and pepper
1 cup diced raw celery
6 tablespoons cooked peas
4 tablespoons diced pickled beetroot
12 oz diced cooked corned beef (350g)

Soften the gelatine in cold water. Then add the boiling stock and stir well until the gelatine is dissolved. Season with Worcester sauce, salt and pepper. When the mixture begins to thicken, add the celery, peas, beetroot and corned beef. Chill until firm and unmould on a bed of lettuce.

Hamburgers

Unless your butcher is a man in whom you can place perfect trust, do not accept mince from the 'minced steak' tray. More often than not the so-called steak is a mixum-gatherum of skinny trimmings from hock, chop and brisket. And since nothing comes out of a bag but what goes into it, hamburgers made with this mince will taste like fried ball-bearings.

Instead, ask him nicely for 1 lb of round steak. And when the steak has been cut and weighed, ask him, still more nicely, to mince it. He may give you a cold look. But a butcher's coldness is quickly forgotten. You have to live with your family.

Classic hamburgers

The real hamburger contains nothing except meat and seasonings. A lb of mince will make 4 thick or 8 thin patties.

Pat the steaks into cakes and fry in a small amount of fat or broil under the grill, about 3 inches from the heat, turning once. Thick hamburgers will take 8 minutes (rare), 12 minutes (medium) or 16 minutes (well done).

Chicken-fried hamburgers
Divide 1 lb (450g) of minced steak into four even patties. Dip into seasoned flour, then into an egg which has been beaten with 2 tablespoons of water. Dip again in flour, before browning on both sides in hot fat. Cover and cook slowly for 20–30 minutes.

To make gravy, remove the cooked hamburgers and add to the fat in the pan 1 tablespoon of seasoned flour blended with 1 cup of milk. Stir until it comes to the boil and boil for 1 minute.

Hamburgers (German)

1 cup breadcrumbs
1¾ pints stock or water (995ml)
1 lb minced steak (450g)
2 well-beaten eggs
1 tablespoon butter or margarine
2 tablespoons chopped onion
3 tablespoons chopped parsley
Salt
¼ teaspoon paprika
½ teaspoon grated lemon rind
1 teaspoon lemon juice
1 teaspoon mushroom catsup
2 tablespoons bacon fat
2 tablespoons flour
2 tablespoons chopped mixed pickles
2 tablespoons chopped parsley

Soak the breadcrumbs in ¼ pint (150ml) of stock or water. Add the minced steak and eggs. Sauté the onions in butter until light brown and add to the steak, with the chopped parsley, salt, paprika, lemon rind and juice, and Worcester sauce. Mix well and shape into 2-inch balls with floured hands. Boil 1½ pints of stock, drop in the meat balls, cover and simmer for 15 minutes. Remove with a fish slice.

Melt the bacon fat, stir in the flour and cook until brown.
Add gradually about ¾ pint of stock, boil, stirring well and add
the pickles and parsley. Reheat the meat balls in the gravy, and
serve surrounded by a thick rampart of fluffy mashed
potatoes sprinkled thickly with browned breadcrumbs.

Hamburger loaf with mushroom stuffing

1 lb minced steak (450g)
1 beaten egg
2 tablespoons milk (30ml)
2 tablespoons tomato ketchup (30ml)
1 teaspoon dry mustard
Salt and pepper

The sauce:

2 oz butter or margarine (50g)
4 oz sliced mushrooms (110g)
2 tablespoons chopped onion
1 teaspoon lemon juice
2 cups breadcrumbs
1 tablespoon chopped parsley
Salt and pepper

To the steak, add the egg and other ingredients. Pack half of
the mixture into a well-greased pie dish. To make the stuffing:
Melt the butter over a low heat, add the mushrooms, onion
and lemon juice and sauté for 3 minutes. Add the crumbs and
seasoning. Spread this stuffing over the meat, then add the
remainder of the meat. Bake for 1 hour at 375° (gas mark 5).
Turn out into a hot dish, sprinkle with browned breadcrumbs,
garnish with chopped parsley and sliced tomato and serve with
rich brown gravy.

Hamburger loaves (individual)

1 lb minced steak (450g)
4 oz chopped onion (110g)
8 oz breadcrumbs (225g)
1 teaspoon Worcester sauce
¼ cup cream or top of bottle
¼ teaspoon dry mustard
Salt and pepper
Streaky rashers

Combine all the ingredients and shape into 8 small loaves. Wrap a streaky rasher around each, and bake for 30 minutes at 400° (gas mark 6).

Hamburger sausage

1 lb minced steak (450g)
½ pint scalded milk (275ml)
1 cup brown breadcrumbs
1 medium chopped onion
1 teaspoon mixed herbs
Salt and pepper
2 beaten eggs
1 cup white breadcrumbs
3 tablespoons fat

Add the milk to the brown breadcrumbs. When cool, beat smooth with a fork. Add the steak, onion, herbs, and season to taste. Then add the eggs, keeping back about 1 tablespoon. With floured hands, shape the mixture like a sausage, brush with beaten egg and roll in white breadcrumbs. Melt the fat and, when really hot, brown the meat sausage on all sides. Bake for 1½ hours at 375° (gas mark 5), basting now and then. Serve with tomato sauce or brown gravy.

Hamburger stew

1 lb minced steak (450g)
1 large chopped onion
1 cup breadcrumbs
Salt and pepper
1 beaten egg
2 tablespoons flour
2 tablespoons fat
Hot water or stock
6 sliced carrots
8 halved potatoes
1 cup peas
Chopped parsley

Mix together the steak, onion, breadcrumbs, salt and pepper, and then the beaten egg. Form into patties, roll in flour and brown quickly in fat. Sprinkle the rest of the flour on the meat, add hot water to cover, bring to the boil and simmer for 35 minutes. Add the carrots and potatoes and simmer for another 20 to 25 minutes. Add the peas and simmer until the vegetables are tender. Sprinkle with parsley.

Hamburger stew with dumplings	1½ lb minced steak (675g) 1 tablespoon chopped onion Salt and pepper 2 tablespoons fat 1 tablespoon flour 1 medium tin tomato soup 1 dessertspoon tomato ketchup 1 pint hot stock or water (570ml) 1 recipe plain dumplings

Mix the meat, onion, salt and pepper. Shape lightly into small cakes and sear in hot fat until browned on both sides. Remove the cakes from the pan, stir in flour, and add the tomato soup, ketchup and water. Return the cakes to the pan and drop 1 tablespoon of dumpling mixture on top of each. Cook uncovered for 6 minutes, then cover tightly and cook for another 10 minutes.

Hamburger T-bone steak	1 lb minced steak (450g) 1 tablespoon chopped onion ¼ pint milk (150ml) ½ cup breadcrumbs Salt and pepper Fat for cooking

Mix together all the ingredients and shape like a T-bone steak. Quickly brown in hot fat on both sides, reduce the heat and continue cooking until done to your taste.

Spiced beef

In many parts of the country, spiced beef is one of the great delicacies of the Christmas season.

Spiced beef	1 teaspoon each allspice, cinnamon, cloves 1 bay leaf Salt and pepper

2 cups cider
Water
3 lb topside beef (1350g)
2 chopped onions
2 chopped carrots
1 chopped turnip
2 stalks chopped celery

Mix the spices, bay leaf, salt and pepper with the cider. Place the meat in a large dish, pour the marinade over it and let it stand for 12 hours, turning twice. Then place it in a heavy saucepan. Combine the marinade with sufficient water to cover, bring to the boil and pour over the meat. Cover closely and simmer for 3 hours.

Spiced beef can be eaten cold, or served hot with this sauce: Sauté the onions, carrots, turnips and celery in butter or dripping. Add ¾ pint (425ml) of liquor from the meat and simmer for about 10 minutes or until they are tender.

Spiced beef, moulded

2 lb lean beef (900g)
1 cracked knuckle of veal
Bouquet garni
1 tablespoon vinegar
Water
½ teaspoon each allspice, cloves, mace
Salt and pepper
¼ teaspoon dry mustard

Cut the beef into 1-inch cubes and place in a large saucepan, with the knuckle of veal and bouquet garni. Add the vinegar and just enough water to cover. Simmer (covered) for 3 hours, or until meat is very tender. When partially cooked, remove the meat from the stock and chop roughly. Skim off the fat and strain.

Add to the stock, spices, mustard, salt and pepper. Bring to the boil, add the meat, heat thoroughly, then chill. Stir to distribute the meat, turn into a mould and chill until firm. Serve garnished with sliced tomatoes.

Note: If the sauce is too watery, drain off some before chilling.

Steak

Steak and kidney pie (1)

1½ lb chuck or round steak (675g)
4 oz veal or lamb kidney (110g)
1 large chopped onion
3 tablespoons dripping
1½ pints stock (850ml)
½ bay leaf
1 small chopped carrot
1 stalk chopped celery
½ teaspoon Worcester sauce
Salt and pepper
1 tablespoon flour
8 oz flaky or shortcrust pastry (225g)

Cut the beef into 1½-inch cubes. Trim the membrane from the kidney and slice thinly. Brown the onion in the fat, add the steak and kidney and stir until all the cubes are well coated and lightly browned. Add the boiling stock and bay leaf. Cover and simmer until the meat is tender (about 2 hours). For the last 30 minutes of cooking, add the celery and carrot. Thicken the stock with *beurre manié*, and season. Place the stew in a large baking dish and cover while hot with the pastry. Make a hole in the top and bake for 20 minutes at 450° (gas mark 8).

For added flavour, reduce the stock by about 3 tablespoons and add 3 tablespoons of dry red wine.

Steak and kidney pie (2)

1 lb round steak (450g)
8 oz beef kidney (110g)
2 oz streaky rashers (50g)
1 tablespoon flour
Salt and pepper
1 tablespoon butter or dripping
1 pint stock or water (570ml)
2 oz chopped mushrooms (50g)
1 dessertspoon chopped onion
1 dessertspoon chopped parsley
8 oz shortcrust pastry (225g)

Cut the steak into cubes, trim the membrane from the kidney and slice thinly. Chop the bacon. Season the flour and sauté the meat in the fat until lightly browned. Add the stock, mushrooms, onion and parsley. Cover and simmer slowly until the meat is tender. When cold, turn into a pie dish and cover with the pastry. Flute the edges, make a hole in the centre, and trim with pastry leaves. Brush with beaten egg and bake for 25 minutes at 450° (gas mark 8).

Steak and kidney pudding

1 teaspoon baking powder
1 cup flour
Salt
1 cup breadcrumbs
1 cup chopped beef suet
1 lb round steak (450g)
4 oz beef kidney (110g)
4 oz sliced mushrooms (110g)
½ pint stock or water (275ml)

Sieve together baking powder, flour and salt. Mix with the breadcrumbs and suet and make a stiff paste with cold water. Roll out two-thirds of the paste ⅛ inch thick and line a pudding bowl. Trim the kidney and cut it and the steak into small cubes. Roll the meat and mushrooms in seasoned flour, place in the pudding bowl and add the stock. Roll the remaining paste to make a lid. Moisten the edges and press together, tie down with greased paper and steam for 3 hours.

Stuffed steak rolls

1 rasher streaky bacon
1 cup breadcrumbs
1 teaspoon chopped parsley
1 teaspoon chopped onion
½ teaspoon dried herbs
¼ teaspoon grated lemon rind
Salt and pepper
1 beaten egg
1 lb round steak (450g)
1 sliced onion
½ pint stock (275ml)
8 oz sliced tomatoes (225g)

Make a stuffing by combining the finely chopped rasher, breadcrumbs, parsley, onion, herbs, lemon rind and seasoning. Bind with the beaten egg. Cut the steak into strips about 4 inch x 2 inch, and flatten with a rolling pin. Spread the stuffing on the steak slices, roll up and tie securely. Cover the bottom of a casserole with a sliced onion and place the meat rolls on top. Add the stock, cover and bake for about 1 hour at 325° (gas mark 3) until the meat is tender. Skim the liquid and strain. Add the tomatoes and simmer until they are soft. Rub through a sieve, season well and serve around the rolls.

Steak Stroganoff

1 lb round steak (450g)
1 tablespoon grated onion
3 tablespoons butter or margarine
4 oz sliced mushrooms (110g)
Salt and pepper
$\frac{1}{8}$ teaspoon nutmeg
$\frac{1}{2}$ cup sour cream

Cut the steak into portions and pound until it is very thin. Sauté the onion in 1 tablespoon of fat for 2 minutes, then sauté the steak quickly for about 5 minutes, turning it to brown evenly. Remove and keep hot. Add to the pan the rest of the butter and sauté the mushrooms. Add the steak, salt, pepper and nutmeg. Stir in the cream but do not allow to boil.

If you cannot get sour cream, use top of the bottle and 1 teaspoon lemon juice.

Steak toad-in-the-hole

1 beaten egg
$\frac{1}{3}$ pint milk (190ml)
4 oz flour (110g)
Salt and pepper
$\frac{1}{4}$ teaspoon mixed herbs
1 lb round steak (450g)

Make a batter with the egg, milk and flour. Add the mixed herbs and season. Cube the steak. Pour half of the batter into a greased and heated fireproof dish and bake for about 7 minutes at 400° (gas mark 6) until the batter begins to set.

Now add the steak and pour the remainder of the batter over it. Return to the oven and bake until golden brown (about 20 minutes). Reduce the heat to 325° (gas mark 3) and cook for another 30 minutes.

Stuffed steak

1½ lb round steak (675g)
2 cups parsley and thyme stuffing
1 beaten egg
2 oz butter or margarine (50g)
1 tablespoon flour
Salt and pepper
1 pint stock or water (570ml)
3 sliced carrots
3 chopped onions
8 small potatoes

Beat the steak with a rolling pin until thin and flat. Spread the stuffing on it, roll up and secure with skewers or string. Sear quickly in hot fat and place in a casserole. Brown the flour in the fat, season, blend in the stock, bring to the boil and pour over the steak. Cover and cook at 325° (gas mark 3). After 1 hour, place the carrots and onions around the side of the casserole and cover the steak with the potatoes. Cover and cook until the vegetables are tender (about 1–1½ hours).

Swiss steak

2 tablespoons flour
Salt and pepper
1 lb round steak (450g)
1 tablespoon bacon fat
1 medium sliced onion
8 oz tomatoes (225g)
½ pint stock or water (275ml)

Season 1 tablespoon of flour with salt and pepper, and pound into both sides of the steak. Sear the steak quickly in hot fat and remove to a casserole. Sauté the onions, add to the steak, and cover with the tomatoes. Stir 1 tablespoon of flour into the fat in the pan, and when brown add the stock and season to taste. Boil, stirring constantly. Pour into the casserole, cover and cook for 2½ hours at 300° (gas mark 2).

Veal

Veal (meat of the calf) is at its best in summer. The fat should be white and the lean pale pink. For best flavour, choose veal that is moderately fat.

Loin, shoulder or leg are roasted, sometimes boned and stuffed. Cutlets (from the neck or loin) and escalopes (from the fillet or leg) are fried in egg and breadcrumbs. Chops (from the chump end of the loin) are grilled or fried.

Blanquette of veal

1½ lb veal (675g)
2 pints stock or water (1140ml)
6 stalks diced celery
Bouquet garni
2 cloves
Salt and pepper
½ teaspoon grated nutmeg
8 small onions
2 oz butter or margarine (50g)
2 oz flour (50g)
2 egg yolks
1 tablespoon lemon juice
1 tablespoon sherry

Cut the veal in 2-inch squares. Combine and bring slowly to the boil, the stock, celery, bouquet garni and seasonings. Drop the meat, piece by piece, into the pot, taking care that the stock does not go off the boil. Reduce the heat, cover and simmer for about 1 hour or until the meat is tender, adding the onions during the last ½ hour of cooking. Remove meat and onions and keep hot. Strain the stock and skim. Blend the butter and flour, stir in slowly 2 cups of the stock, season to taste, and continue stirring until smooth and boiling. Remove from the heat, beat in the egg yolks, and stir until thick, but do not boil. Remove from the heat and add the lemon juice and sherry. Arrange the meat and onions on a platter inside a border of mashed potatoes or rice. Pour the sauce over.

Creamed veal

1½ lb veal (675g)
3 tablespoons flour
Salt and pepper

2 tablespoons butter or margarine
¾ pint milk or half milk and cream
   (425ml)
4 oz button mushrooms (110g)

Trim the veal, cut into small pieces and pound until thin. Roll the pieces in 1 tablespoon of seasoned flour, and sauté in butter. Place in a casserole. Add the rest of the flour to the pan, stir until lightly browned, add the milk, and season. Bring to the boil and cook for 3 minutes. Add the mushrooms to the casserole, pour over the sauce, and cook for 1 hour at 325° (gas mark 3).

Curried veal

2 oz flour (50g)
Salt
2 tablespoons curry powder
2 lb veal (900g)
2 tablespoons butter or margarine
2 large chopped onions
1 large sliced apple
2 tablespoons seedless raisins
2 tablespoons shredded coconut
2 tablespoons chopped walnuts
2 tablespoons brown sugar
1 small sliced lemon
1 clove garlic
1 pint water (570ml)

Mix the flour, salt and curry powder. Trim and cut the veal into small squares and dredge thickly with the flour. Sauté the onions until golden brown in butter, then remove and brown the meat on all sides. Put it into a stewpan with the onions, apples, raisins, coconut, walnuts, brown sugar, lemons and minced garlic. Add the water, bring to the boil and simmer gently until the meat is tender (about 1½ hours). Serve with plain boiled rice. Serve separately chutney, mustard, pickles.

Escalopes in cider

1 lb veal (450g)
1 tablespoon flour
Salt and pepper
2 tablespoons olive oil

1 clove garlic
¼ pint cider or dry white wine (150ml)
¼ pint water (150ml)
2 teaspoons lemon juice

Cut the veal into fingers, ¼ inch thick, and roll in the seasoned flour. Heat the oil in a heavy pan and sauté the minced garlic. Remove the garlic and brown the floured veal. Add the cider, water and lemon juice. Cover and simmer for 30 minutes.

Escalopes Parmesan
Trim and flatten veal escalopes, and season with salt, pepper and paprika. Dip into grated Parmesan cheese and fry until light brown in butter (3 minutes on each side).

Pressed veal

2½ lb breast or neck of veal (1125g)
8 oz unsalted streaky pork (225g)
Salt and pepper
1 sliced onion/1 stalk of celery

Put the veal into a saucepan with the pork and add boiling water to cover. Cook for 5 minutes, skim, and simmer (covered) for about 2 hours or until the meat is very tender. Season when half done. Remove the meat from the bones, and mince finely with the onion and celery. Return to the stock and simmer until thick but moist, stirring constantly. Pack into a bowl and chill thoroughly. When ready, cut in thin slices.

Roast veal
Loin, shoulder or leg can all be roasted. Allow 25 minutes per lb. Place the meat in a 400° (gas mark 6) oven, and after 15 minutes reduce to 350° (gas mark 4). Baste frequently.

Veal and ham pie

1 tablespoon flour
Salt and pepper
1 teaspoon mixed herbs
1 lb veal (450g)
8 oz raw ham (225g)
12 oz puff pastry (350g)
1 egg

Season the flour with salt, pepper and herbs. Dice the veal and ham and roll in the flour. Place in a pie dish, and add cold water to three-quarters fill the dish. Brush the rim with water, and cover with pastry rolled ¼ inch thick. Make 2 cuts in the lid to allow the steam to escape. Brush with beaten egg and cook at 475° (gas mark 9) for 20 minutes, then reduce the heat to 375° (gas mark 5) and cook for another 15 minutes.

Veal roll	**3 lb breast of veal (1350g)**
	2 cups stuffing
	Fat for roasting
	1 tablespoon flour

Place the boned veal skin side downwards. Spread with stuffing, roll up, skewer or tie, and sprinkle with flour. Melt the fat in a roasting tin, put the veal into it, and bake at 450° (gas mark 8) for 15 minutes. Then reduce the heat to 375° (gas mark 5) and continue baking for 1¼ hours. Serve with gravy.

Veal roll, glazed
Veal roll can be served cold, covered with a glaze. Simmer the bones for 1½ hours in cold water to cover, with 1 chopped carrot, 1 sliced onion, salt and pepper. Pour away the fat from the roasting tin, leaving brown sediment. Add the strained liquor from the bones and boil rapidly until reduced to less than ½ pint. When cold, pour over the meat.

Wiener schnitzel (Viennese escalopes)	**4 escalopes veal**
	1 tablespoon flour
	Salt and pepper
	2 oz breadcrumbs (50g)
	1 egg
	Butter for frying

Beat the escalopes to ¼ inch thick, and pound into them the seasoned flour. Bind the breadcrumbs with the egg, dip the escalopes into the mixture and fry in butter over moderate heat, allowing about 4 minutes to each side. Pour the remainder of the butter over the escalopes and garnish with capers, lemon slice and grated cooked egg white.

Mutton and lamb

Mutton is in season all the ear round. Fat should be white and firm, lean should be dark red.

Lamb is in season in late spring and early summer — and should not be more than 3 months old. Fat should be white, the lean red but paler than mutton. Cuts and cooking methods are the same as for mutton.

Baking

Cuts: Chops.

Creole chops	4 thick chops
	1 tablespoon flour
	Salt and pepper
	Fat
	1 large tin tomato soup
	1 large chopped onion
	1 chopped green pepper
	3 tablespoons breadcrumbs

Trim the chops and render the fat from them. Season the flour, dredge the chops with it, and brown in hot fat (either the rendered fat or butter or margarine). Place in a baking tin, and pour around a tin of tomato soup mixed with the same amount of water. Add the pepper and onion. Cover and bake for $1\frac{1}{4}$ hours in 375° (gas mark 5). After an hour, remove the cover, sprinkle the chops with breadcrumbs and bake uncovered for the last 15 minutes.

Lamb barbecue	3 lb breast of lamb (1350g)
	2 cloves garlic
	5 tablespoons vinegar
	Salt and pepper
	1 teaspoon each paprika and mustard
	1 tablespoon Worcester sauce
	2 tablespoons water

Cut the lamb into 2-inch squares. Place on rack in a roasting tin, and cook for 30 minutes at 425° (gas mark 7). Pour off fat and remove the rack. Mix the garlic with the vinegar, salt and pepper, paprika, prepared mustard, sauce and water. Pour over the meat in the pan. Peeled medium-sized potatoes may be added. Reduce the heat to 375° (gas mark 5), cover and bake for 1 hour. Uncover and bake for another 15 minutes or until meat and potatoes are browned.

Stuffed chops

4 thick chops
4 tablespoons breadcrumbs
Salt and pepper
$\frac{1}{4}$ teaspoon nutmeg
$\frac{1}{2}$ teaspoon grated lemon rind
1 teaspoon chopped parsley
1 dessertspoon chopped onion
1 beaten egg
4 rashers streaky bacon

Trim the chops and make a cut down the side of each. Mix together the breadcrumbs, salt, pepper, nutmeg, lemon rind, parsley and onion, and bind with the beaten egg. Divide the stuffing between each chop, tie with thread and wrap each in a slice of bacon. Placed on a greased tin and cook for about 25 minutes at 400° (gas mark 6). Turn when half cooked. Serve with tomato purée and green peas.

Braising

Cuts: Breast (cooked with or without boning), chops, shank (have the butcher remove bone and excess fat), and shoulder.
Cooking: Method is the same as for beef.

Braised breast of mutton

2 lb breast of mutton (900g)
2 cups celery stuffing
Salt and pepper
$\frac{1}{2}$ pint stock or water (275ml)
1 sliced onion

Wipe the meat with a damp cloth, season, and spread with the celery stuffing. Roll up, secure with string or skewers, and sear quickly in a greased baking tin. Add stock, cover and braise at 325° (gas mark 3) or until meat is tender. During the last 30 minutes, add the onion and finish cooking, uncovered.

Braised lamb shanks

4 lamb or mutton shanks
2 tablespoons seasoned flour
2 tablespoons dripping or butter
$\frac{3}{4}$ pint stock (425ml)
Salt and pepper
$\frac{1}{2}$ bay leaf

Roll the shanks in seasoned flour. Melt the fat in a stewpan and sear the shanks on all sides until deep brown. Pour off the fat. Add the stock, salt, pepper and bay leaf, cover the pan closely and simmer for 3 hours; or cook in the oven in a covered casserole.

For the last 30 minutes of cooking, diced vegetables — tomatoes, carrots, onions, potatoes — can be added. Before serving thicken the sauce.

Braised mutton and celery

1 head chopped celery
1 chopped carrot
1 sliced onion
1 oz butter or margarine (25g)
$1\frac{1}{2}$ lb lean mutton (675g)
Salt and pepper
$\frac{1}{4}$ pint stock or water (150ml)

Sauté the vegetables in the melted fat for about 5 minutes. Place in a casserole. Trim the mutton, cut in fingers and sear quickly in the pan. Add to the vegetables, season and add the stock (8 oz of sliced tomatoes may also be added). Cover and cook for $1\frac{1}{2}$ hours at 375° (gas mark 5). Serve with baked potatoes.

Braised shoulder of lamb

$2\frac{1}{2}$-3 lb shoulder of lamb
** (1125–1350g)**
1 clove of garlic
3 cups parsley and thyme stuffing
1 pint stock or water (570ml)
3 cups diced mixed vegetables
** (carrots, turnips, celery, onions)**
1 tablespoon flour
Salt and pepper

Get the butcher to bone a shoulder of lamb. Rub with a clove of garlic, spread the stuffing on the meat, roll up and secure with string. Place in a dry stew pan on a rack in a hot oven for 15 minutes. Add the bones and ½ pint of stock. Reduce the heat to 350° (gas mark 4), cover the pan, and cook for 45 minutes. Put the diced vegetables into the pan and add the rest of the stock. Cover and cook for another hour. Glaze the meat and vegetables by removing the cover and cooking uncovered for a further 10 minutes. Remove meat and vegetables. Prepare gravy by boiling the liquid until reduced by one quarter. Strain, thicken with *beurre manié*, and simmer for 3 minutes. Season to taste.

Frying and grilling

Cuts: Loin chops, cutlets.

Cooking: For grilling, turn on the grill 5 minutes before you need it. Rub chops with salad oil or melted butter and sprinkle with pepper and salt. Place on grill, cook for 3 minutes on each side, then reduce the heat for the remainder of the cooking time. A chop 1½ inches thick will need 5 minutes on each side. Turn with tongs or fish slice, never with a fork.

Breaded cutlets

8 lamb cutlets
1 tablespoon flour
Salt and pepper
1 beaten egg
1 tablespoon water (15ml)
1 cup breadcrumbs
Fat for frying

Trim the cutlets, beat lightly with a rolling pin to flatten, and dredge in seasoned flour. Mix the egg with the water, and dip the chops in this, making sure they are completely coated. Coat thickly with breadcrumbs and fry for four minutes on each side in hot fat.

Epicure lamb chops

1 teaspoon each chopped sage, parsley, spring onion
Salt and pepper

2 lb cutlets from best end neck of lamb
or young mutton (900g)
1 egg
4 tablespoons breadcrumbs
2 oz butter or margarine (50g)

Mix together the sage, parsley and finely chopped onion, and season. Trim the cutlets, dip into the beaten egg, then the herb mixture, then into the breadcrumbs. Fry until golden-brown in butter.

Italian cutlets

6 lamb or mutton cutlets
¾ pint milk (425ml)
1 tablespoon chopped parsley
4 tablespoons breadcrumbs
1 beaten egg
1 tablespoon water
3 tablespoons butter or margarine
2 tablespoons flour
1 dessertspoon lemon juice
Salt and pepper

Trim the cutlets, and place in a saucepan with the milk and parsley. Cover and simmer slowly for 1 hour. Drain the chops, roll in breadcrumbs, then in egg lightly beaten with water. Roll again in crumbs and sauté in two tablespoons of butter until lightly browned on both sides. Keep hot while making the sauce. Add the remaining butter to the pan, gradually stir in the flour, stirring constantly, until it is lightly browned. Add the milk in which the cutlets were simmered, cook for 5 minutes, then add the remainder of the beaten egg, and stir for another minute. Remove from the heat, add lemon juice, and season. Strain this sauce over the cutlets.

Lamb patties

1 lb lamb or mutton (450g)
Salt and pepper
6 rashers streaky bacon
3 halved tomatoes

Mince the mutton, season and form into 6 patties. Wrap a rasher of bacon around each and fasten with small toothpicks.

Broil for 8 minutes on each side. When browned, top each patty with a half tomato, brush with fat from the pan and continue broiling until the tomato is cooked.

Savoury chops	**4 lamb chops** **1 clove garlic** **1 oz butter or margarine (25g)** **1 sprig each parsley, thyme, and tarragon, or $\frac{1}{2}$ teaspoon dried herbs** **Salt and pepper** **2 tablespoons breadcrumbs**

Trim the chops and rub them over with a cut clove of garlic. Melt the butter, mix with it the chopped or dried herbs, and season. Coat each chop with the herb mixture, then dip them into the breadcrumbs. Grill the chops, allowing about 5 minutes to each side for a chop $1\frac{1}{2}$ inches thick. Turn frequently with a grilling tongs.

Roasting

Cuts: Best end of neck, breast, leg, loin, saddle and shank.
Cooking: For mutton, allow 20 minutes to the lb and 20 minutes over. For lamb, allow 25 minutes to the lb and 25 minutes over. Preheat the oven to 450° (gas mark 8) and cook at this heat for 30 minutes, then reduce to 350° (gas mark 4).

Roast lamb

The greatest treat of the year is the first roast of spring lamb, delicate, succulent and tender. Although cheaper than the leg, the forequarter, being fatter, is better flavoured. Whatever joint you choose, remember that lamb requires slow, even and long cooking. Unlike beef, which may and should be served rare and underdone in the centre, lamb is perfectly cooked only when evenly browned on the surface and uniformly roasted throughout.

If you like garlic, insert a few slivers in the flesh. Rosemary also enhances the flavour of lamb.

Note: The French like *their* lamb slightly pink in the centre.

Roast lamb (crown)

A crown roast of lamb is usually prepared from the loin. Two chops are allowed for each person — about 3 to 4 lb for 6 persons. The meat must be kept in one piece. Get the butcher to chop well down between each bone. Trim each chop bone as for cutlets but do not separate them. Now roll the joint in the form of a crown, the meat outside and the bone part inside. With thread, tie a thin strip of fat bacon round each cutlet bone, so that it will not char in the cooking.

A crown roast may be stuffed with ordinary poultry stuffing to which have been added the minced trimmings from the meat. Or it may be cooked empty, and filled when cooked with mashed potato sprinkled with parsley, or with a mixture of cooked buttered vegetables such as peas and diced carrots. Or, a cooked cauliflower may be placed in the centre of the crown and topped with a layer of browned buttered crumbs.

Before putting the joint to cook, sprinkle with flour, pepper and salt. Melt a little butter in a baking tin and put in the joint. Cover with buttered paper. Cook in a hot oven at 450° (gas mark 8). After 30 minutes reduce to 350° (gas mark 4). Allow $1\frac{1}{2}$ to $1\frac{3}{4}$ hours roasting, according to the thickness of the cutlets. About 20 minutes before the joint is cooked, remove the paper so that it may be nicely browned. When you take the roast from the oven, remove the strips of fat bacon from the ends of the cutlet bones. Put a cutlet frill around each bone, or impale a small boiled onion on each.

Stewing

Cuts: Breast, scrag end of neck.

Haricot mutton

4 tablespoons haricot beans
2 lb boned breast or neck of mutton
1 oz dripping (25g)
Salt and pepper
2 chopped carrots
2 chopped white turnips
2 sliced onions
Stock or water

Soak the beans overnight. Cut the mutton into small pieces and brown on all sides in the dripping. Put the meat into a casserole and season. Toss the vegetables for about 5 minutes in the fat in which the meat was browned, and add to the meat together with the beans. Barely cover with stock or water. Cover the casserole and cook in a slow oven at 325° (gas mark 3) until the meat is tender (about $2\frac{1}{2}$ hours).

Irish stew

$2\frac{1}{2}$ lb chops from best end of neck
12 oz sliced onions (350g)
12 oz sliced carrots (350g)
3 stalks chopped celery
2 lb sliced potatoes (900g)
Salt and pepper
Stock or water
1 dessertspoon parsley

Trim excess fat from the chops. Place a layer of potatoes in a stewpan and season lightly with salt and pepper. Add a layer of meat and a sprinkling of vegetables. Repeat the layers, finishing with potatoes. Barely cover with stock, and cook (covered) over a very low heat for about $2\frac{1}{2}$ hours or until the meat is tender. Skim away excess fat. Serve sprinkled with parsley.

Lamb hotpot

6 shoulder chops
$1\frac{1}{4}$ tablespoons butter
1 pint milk (570ml)
12 small onions
12 halved potatoes
Salt and pepper

Trim excess fat from the chops and brown in butter in a heavy saucepan. Sauté the onions, then add the milk and potatoes, and season. Cover and simmer until the vegetables are tender (about 30 minutes). Arrange the chops, onions and potatoes on a heated dish and serve with gravy made from the liquid in which the chops were cooked, thickened with a roux made from butter and flour, blended and browned for 3 minutes.

Lamb pilau

3 oz butter or margarine (75g)
8 oz sliced tomatoes (225g)
1 bay leaf
4 tablespoons cooked rice
8 oz diced cooked lamb (225g)
Salt and pepper

Melt 1 oz of butter in a saucepan, add the tomatoes and bay leaf, and barely enough water to keep the tomatoes from burning. Cover and simmer for 20 minutes, then put the purée through a sieve. Melt the remainder of the butter in a heavy pan, add the cooked rice and sauté for 3 minutes, over low heat, stirring constantly. Add the tomato purée, the lamb and enough stock to moisten thoroughly. Season and serve very hot.

Lamb ragout

2 lb breast of lamb (900g)
1 minced clove of garlic
1 tablespoon butter or margarine
$\frac{1}{2}$ pint stock (275ml)
$\frac{1}{2}$ teaspoon each salt and marjoram
12 small onions
1 lb tomatoes (450g)

Cut the meat into 2-inch pieces and trim off any fat. Brown the meat and garlic in butter in a heavy saucepan. Add the stock — it should barely cover the meat. Season with salt and marjoram. Cover and simmer for 45 minutes or until almost tender. Add the onions and simmer for another 45 minutes. Now add the tomatoes cut in wedges, cover and simmer until they are soft. Serve with baked potatoes.

Lamb stew

3 lb neck, breast or shoulder (1350g)
$\frac{1}{2}$ tablespoon flour
Salt and pepper
1 pint stock or water (570ml)
8 small white onions
8 small carrots
$1\frac{1}{2}$ lb potatoes (675g)
1 cup peas

Cut the lamb into small pieces and roll in seasoned flour. Without adding any fat, brown the meat slowly on all sides in a heavy saucepan. Remove the meat and pour off the fat. Return meat to the saucepan, add the stock and bring to the boil. Cover and simmer for 1½ to 2 hours or until meat is almost tender. Add the onions, carrots and potatoes, cover and continue cooking for 25 minutes. Add the peas, then cook for another 5 to 10 minutes. Season.

Lamb and tomato casserole

2 lb cutlets from best end neck of lamb (900g)
1 beaten egg
4 tablespoons breadcrumbs
2 tablespoons dripping or butter
2 sliced carrots
2 small sliced onions
1 dessertspoon chopped parsley
1 tablespoon flour
Salt and pepper
½ pint stock or water (275ml)
1 dessertspoon tomato catsup
1 cup peas

Dip the cutlets into beaten egg and breadcrumbs and brown on each side in hot fat. In a casserole arrange the carrots and onions, and sprinkle with parsley. Place the chops on top. Blend the seasoned flour with the fat in the pan, and when brown, add stock and catsup. Bring to the boil and pour over the chops. Cover and cook for 40 minutes at 375° (gas mark 5). Add the peas, cover and cook for another 5 minutes. Serve with creamed potatoes.

Mutton casserole

2½ lb neck or breast of mutton (1125g)
2 tablespoons flour
Salt and pepper
2 tablespoons bacon fat
½ pint stock or water (275ml)
8 oz tomatoes (225g)
2 cups peas

Trim the mutton, cut into 1 inch cubes and roll in seasoned flour. Sear in bacon fat until well browned. Pour off the excess fat, add stock, cover and simmer for about 1½ hours or until the meat is almost tender. Skim, add the tomatoes and peas and cook for another 30 minutes.

Mutton stew	**1½ lb mutton (675g)** **3 tablespoons flour** **6 streaky rashers** **2 tablespoons fat** **12 small onions** **1 pint stock (570ml)** **1 teaspoon dry mustard** **Salt and pepper**

Trim the meat, cut into 6 pieces and dredge with 2 tablespoons of seasoned flour. Remove rind and bone from the rashers, wrap one around each piece of meat and secure with a toothpick or thread. Melt the fat in a heavy saucepan. Add the meat and onions, and sear until browned, turning them constantly. Remove meat and onions from the pan and pour off all but 1 tablespoon of fat. Stir in the remaining flour and brown, stirring well. Add the stock, stir until smooth and boil, then the meat and onions. Cover and cook for 2 hours over a gentle heat. Season to taste and serve with baked potatoes, carrots and peas.

Pork

Bacon

Boiled bacon

Soak overnight in cold water. Next day change the water, put the bacon in a stewpan with enough cold water to cover, and add a bouquet garni. Bring it slowly to the boil, skim and simmer gently until cooked. Allow approximately 25 minutes to the lb and 25 minutes over (a good test of doneness is when the skin peels easily from the bacon.) Remove the skin, place the bacon on a hot fireproof dish, sprinkle with breadcrumbs, and place under the grill until they brown. Serve with boiled greens, turnips or beetroot and parsley sauce.

Rashers

Back rashers and streaky rashers, whether smoked or pale, can be baked, grilled or fried.

Baked or grilled rashers should be placed on a rack. Baked rashers cook in about 10 minutes at 400° (gas mark 6) and need not be turned. Grilled rashers, placed about 3 inches from the heat, should be turned once.

Ham

Baked ham

Scrape the ham and soak in cold water overnight. Make a paste of flour and water — for every 4 lb of ham, use 1 lb of flour and sufficient water to make a stiff paste. Roll out the paste on a floured board until it is large enough to cover the ham. Wet the ham all over and wrap it in the sheet of paste, wetting the edges so as to form a perfect seal. Place it on a sheet and bake at 425° (gas mark 7). After 20 minutes, reduce the heat to 350° (gas mark 4) and continue baking until the ham is cooked, allowing about 30 minutes to the lb. Strip off crust and rind, and coat the fat with breadcrumbs. If the ham is to be served cold, leave it to cool in its crust.

Note: Foil can be used instead of the paste.

Baked ham, American style
Parboil a 4 lb piece of ham which has been soaked overnight in cold water. Remove the skin, and place the ham on a rack in a baking sheet. Cover the top fat with brown sugar and a little dry mustard. Stud it with whole cloves. Bake in a 425° (gas mark 7) oven for 20 minutes basting it frequently with cider, wine or ginger ale. Dredge with brown sugar. Lower the heat to 350° (gas mark 4) and continue baking for 30 minutes.

Baked ham in milk
Trim the edges of a slice of smoked ham about 1¼ inches thick. Stud the fat with a few cloves. Combine 3 tablespoons of brown sugar and 2 teaspoons prepared mustard. Rub these into both sides of the ham. Sear it on both sides over a quick heat in a little fat. Place in a casserole and pour over ½ cup of rich milk. Cover and bake for 1¼ hours at 350° (gas mark 4). For the last 10 minutes bake it uncovered, basting frequently.

Baked ham with apples
Prepare a thick slice of ham as for baked ham in milk. When seared, place it in a casserole. Cover with thinly sliced apples and brown sugar and sprinkle with ¼ teaspoon cinnamon and ¼ teaspoon ground cloves. Add ½ cup water, fruit juice or cider. Cover and bake for 1¼ hours at 350° (gas mark 4). For the last 10 minutes uncover and baste frequently.

Baked ham with Madeira sauce
Scrape the ham, wash well, and soak overnight in cold water (for at least 12 hours). Next day, place in a pot, cover well with cold water, bring slowly to the boil and simmer gently for 2 hours. Place the ham on a rack in a baking tin, remove skin and stick cloves over the fat surface. Pour 6 oz of honey mixed with 1 glass of Madeira over the ham, and bake at 325° (gas mark 3) for 2½ hours, or until the knuckle bone can be removed.

Baked ham with raisin sauce

Wash and soak the ham. Bake it (uncovered) on a rack at 325° (gas mark 3), allowing 20 minutes to the lb. One hour before it is cooked, take the ham from the oven and remove the rind. Mix together 1 cup of brown sugar, 1 teaspoon dry mustard and 3 tablespoons fine breadcrumbs. Moisten these with 3 tablespoons of cider and spread them on the fat side of the ham. Cut diagonal gashes across the ham in a diamond shape. Stud the fat with cloves. Return it to the oven for 45 minutes. Increase the heat to 425° (gas mark 7) and bake for 15 minutes longer. Serve with raisin and cider sauce.

Barbecued ham

Trim and place in a casserole a 2 lb slice of smoked ham. Combine 2 tablespoons of chopped onion, ½ chopped clove garlic, 2 tablespoons tomato ketchup, 2 tablespoons Worcester sauce, 2 tablespoons cider, 1 large tin tomato soup, 1 teaspoon brown sugar, and ⅛ teaspoon pepper. Pour these ingredients over the ham. Cover the casserole. Bake at 325° (gas mark 3) until tender (about 1 hour).

Boiled ham

Soak ham overnight in cold water. Next day, scrub well and scrape off 'rust' or discoloured parts. Put in a stewpan with cold water to cover. Add a bouquet garni. Bring slowly to the boil, skim well, then simmer until cooked. After it comes to the boil, a ham of 11 lb or under should be given 30 minutes per lb. Over this weight allow 20 minutes per lb and 20 minutes over. When cooked, remove skin and coat with breadcrumbs.

Note: Ham is greatly improved in flavour if simmered in a mixture of half water and cider or ginger ale.

Pork

Pork is at its best from September to April, but the old saying 'Never eat pork unless there's an "r" in the month' does not apply, thanks to modern refrigeration. The skin should be creamy-white and soft, the fat white, and the lean fine-grained and pale pink.

Baked pork chops

6 pork chops
Salt and pepper
¾ pint scalded milk (425ml)
1¾ cups parsley and thyme stuffing
1 beaten egg

Brown the chops quickly on both sides in a hot pan, pressing down the fat selvedge to extract the fat. Place in a large casserole, season and add the milk. Cover and bake at 350° (gas mark 4) for about 45 minutes. Take off the lid and spread on each chop about 2 tablespoons of the stuffing, bound with the egg. Continue baking (uncovered) about 30 minutes longer, or until the stuffing is browned and the milk has been absorbed by the chops.

Braised pork steak

2 pork steaks
1 cup breadcrumb stuffing
1 chopped apple
2 tablespoons butter or margarine
Salt and pepper
2 tablespoons chopped onion
4 streaky rashers
¼ pint stock (150ml)

Split the pork steaks lengthwise, being careful not to cut through. Spread one with the stuffing mixed with the chopped apple. Place the other steak on top and tie securely. Brown on all sides quickly in butter, transfer to a casserole and season. Cover with chopped onion and lay the rashers on top. Add the stock, cover and bake for 1½ hours at 325° (gas mark 3).

Pork pie

1 recipe raised pie pastry
1½ lb lean pork (675g)
Salt and pepper
¼ teaspoon powdered dried sage
1 beaten egg
¾ pint stock (425ml)
1 oz gelatine (25g)

Line a cake tin with two-thirds of the dough. Fill with the pork, cut in cubes and sprinkled with salt, pepper and sage. Cover with pastry lid, make a hole in the top to allow steam to escape, add pastry leaves for decoration, and brush with beaten egg. Bake for 2 hours at 375° (gas mark 5). Heat the stock, dissolve the gelatine in it, and when cold and almost set, pour it into the pie through the hole in top.

Pork spare ribs	1½ lb spare ribs (675g) Water 1½ lb sliced potatoes (675g) 2 chopped carrots 8 oz sliced onions (225g) Salt and pepper ½ teaspoon dried sage ¼ teaspoon dry mustard

Cover the ribs with cold water, bring slowly to the boil, skim and simmer until the meat is almost tender. Remove the meat from ribs and chop. Place a layer of potatoes in a casserole, add a layer of meat, carrots and onions. Season with salt, pepper, sage and mustard. Repeat the layers, finishing with potatoes. Add 1 pint of the stock in which the ribs were cooked, cover and cook for 1½ hours at 375° (gas mark 5). For the last 25 minutes of cooking, remove the lid to let the potatoes brown.

Roast pork
Cuts: Fillet, leg, loin, pork steak.
Cooking: Allow 25 minutes to the lb and 25 minutes over. Brush the skin with salad oil to ensure that crackling will be crisp. Place in a hot oven at 475° (gas mark 9) for 10 minutes, then reduce to 375° (gas mark 5). Baste occasionally to keep moist.

Rolled and stuffed pork	2 lb pork belly (900g) 8 oz sausage stuffing (225g) A little salad oil Dripping

Place the meat, skin downwards, on table and spread with

sausage stuffing. Roll up and tie, score the skin and brush with salad oil. Place pork in a baking tin or casserole containing melted dripping. Cover and bake for 1½ hours at 450° (gas mark 8). Uncover and bake for a further 20 minutes. Serve with brown gravy and apple sauce.

Sausages

Sausage and lentil casserole

8 oz lentils (225g)
2 pints water (1140ml)
Bouquet garni
1 onion stuck with cloves
1 tablespoon flour
1 oz butter or margarine (25g)
1 lb sausages (450g)

Soak the lentils overnight (unless they are the quick cooking variety). Boil the water, add the bouquet garni, the onion and the lentils. Simmer gently until they are tender. Drain. Make a roux by browning the flour in the melted butter. Put the lentils through a sieve, add this purée to the roux and season. Place in an ovenproof dish. Simmer the sausages for 10 minutes in boiling water, then arrange on the lentil purée. Bake (uncovered) at 400° (gas mark 6) until the sausages are brown.

Sausages with onion sauce

1 lb sausages (450g)
2 tablespoons flour
1 tablespoon bacon or other fat
8 oz onions (225g)
1 clove garlic
½ pint stock (275ml)
2 tablespoons tomato ketchup
Salt and pepper

Skin the sausages, form into flat cakes, dust with half of the flour and fry until brown in the fat. Remove and keep warm. Sauté the onions and garlic in the fat, and when light brown stir in the rest of the flour and brown slightly. Add the stock, the tomato ketchup and seasoning. Bring to the boil and simmer for 5 minutes. Pour over the sausage cakes.

Sausage pancakes

4 oz flour (110g)
1 egg
½ pint milk (275ml)
Salt and pepper
1 lb sausages (450g)

Make a batter with the flour, egg and milk, and season and make into as many small pancakes as there are sausages. Fry the sausages. Place a sausage on each pancake and top with a spoonful of apple sauce.

Sausages in potatoes

1 lb mashed potatoes (450g)
1 teaspoon chopped onion
1 teaspoon chopped parsley
1 egg yolk
Salt and pepper
12 sausages
1 whole egg
1 tablespoon milk

Combine the mashed potatoes, onion, parsley and egg yolk. Season. Cook the sausages and encase each in mashed potatoe. Coat the rolls with breadcrumbs, then dip in the beaten whole egg which has been diluted with the milk. Dip again in the breadcrumbs. Heat the fat to 375° (gas mark 5) and fry the croquettes until golden-brown.

Sausage pudding

2 rashers
4 oz breadcrumbs (110g)
1 tablespoon tomato ketchup
2 tablespoons stock or gravy
1 teaspoon chopped parsley
1 lb sausage meat (450g)
Salt and pepper

Dice the bacon and mix with the breadcrumbs, parsley, ketchup and gravy. Add the sausage meat (if sausages are used they must be skinned). Put the mixture in a well-greased baking tin and bake for 30 minutes at 375° (gas mark 5). Turn on to a hot dish and serve with tomato sauce.

Sausage ring

3 tablespoons fried breadcrumbs
1 lb sausage meat (450g)
¾ cup breadcrumbs
2 tablespoons chopped parsley
1 tablespoon chopped onion
1 beaten egg

Grease a 7-inch ring mould. Put the breadcrumbs on the bottom, and top with all the other ingredients which have been well mixed. Bake for 30 minutes at 350° (gas mark 4), draining the fat away after 15 minutes. When cooked, invert carefully on to a hot dish. Fill the centre with buttered peas and carrots or with scrambled eggs.

Sausage toad-in-hole

4 oz flour (110g)
1 egg
½ pint milk (275ml)
Salt
1 lb sausages (450g)
Fat for frying

Make a batter with the flour, egg and milk, and season. Simmer the sausages for 10 minutes in boiling water, then drain. Grease a shallow fireproof dish with the fat and heat. Pour into it enough batter to form a thin coating over the bottom. Put into a 450° oven (gas mark 8) for 4 minutes to set. Arrange the sausages on the batter and pour the rest of it over them. Return to the oven for 25 minutes. Reduce to 350° (gas mark 4) and bake for another 15 minutes.

Note: To remove sausage skins easily, hold them for a couple of minutes under the cold tap, then slit them; the skins will slip off.

Variety meats

Heart, liver, sweetbreads, tongue, kidneys, brains and tripe are known as variety meats (offal is the trade name). They have a higher nutritional value than the more expensive cuts and should appear more often on our menus.

Baked heart

Trim the heart, cutting away sinews, etc., to make a pocket. Wash well in cold salted water and pat dry. Season inside and out with pepper and salt. Stuff the heart with your favourite breadcrumb stuffing and stitch or tie securely. Place it in a deep casserole and pour over it 2 cups of brown gravy. Place over the heart 4 slices of fat bacon. Cover and bake at 350° (gas mark 4) until tender.

A beef heart may take from 3 to 4 hours, a veal heart 2 hours, a sheep heart 1 hour.

Brawn

Prepare a pig's head by singeing where necessary, removing unsightly portions. If very salt, steep overnight in cold water. Next day cut it into 4 pieces, put into a heavy saucepan, and add a wineglass of cider, 2 bay leaves, 8 peppercorns and 6 cloves. Add sufficient cold water barely to cover, and simmer for 2 hours, or until the flesh falls away from the bones. Strain off the liquor into another saucepan and boil rapidly (uncovered) until it is reduced to a pint. Pack the meat into a bowl, pour over it the reduced liquor, and leave to cool. When cold and firm, scrape off any fat which may have settled on top and turn out the brawn on to a dish.

Kidneys

Wash the kidneys, split in half lengthways, remove the white centres and tubes, and soak from $\frac{1}{2}$ to 2 hours in enough cold, slightly salted water to cover (the length of time will depend on the size and age of the kidneys). This preliminary soaking will eliminate the unpleasant odour sometimes noticeable when pork kidneys are cooking. After soaking, drain the kidneys and pat dry with a cloth. If very old and large, put in cold water after soaking, bring slowly to the boil and then drain.

Breaded kidneys

6 small pork kidneys
1 slightly beaten egg
Water
$\frac{1}{2}$ tablespoon chopped onion
Salt and pepper
1 cup breadcrumbs
2 tablespoons butter or bacon fat

Halve prepared kidneys. Mix the beaten egg with 1 tablespoon of water, add the onion and season. Dip each kidney half in this mixture and roll in breadcrumbs. Brown in butter, add about $\frac{1}{2}$ cup of water, cover and simmer over low heat for about 20 minutes, turning several times. Place, cut side down, in a greased casserole and baste with fat from pan. Bake (uncovered) at 450° (gas mark 8) for 20 minutes.

Grilled kidneys
Prepare the kidneys and halve them. Brush with melted fat or oil and either fry or grill for 12 minutes, browning well on both sides (8 minutes will be sufficient for small and tender kidneys). When cooked, place on a hot dish, dot with butter and garnish with parsley.

Kidney patties

4 pork kidneys
2 teaspoons vinegar
4 tablespoons chopped celery
1 chopped onion
2 tablespoons butter or bacon fat
2 tablespoons milk (30ml)
1 beaten egg
2 tablespoons breadcrumbs
$\frac{1}{2}$ teaspoon Worcester sauce
$\frac{1}{4}$ teaspoon dried herbs
Salt and pepper

Chop the prepared kidneys finely and sprinkle with vinegar. Sauté the celery and onion in butter for 3 minutes. Remove from the heat, and add the kidneys, milk, egg, breadcrumbs,

Worcester sauce, herbs and seasoning. Heat the pan, brush it with butter and drop the mixture by spoonfuls on the pan. Brown lightly on both sides, cover and let the patties cook for about 20 minutes. Serve with tomato purée and boiled rice.

Kidney ragout

6 small pork kidneys
3 tablespoons flour
3 tablespoons butter or bacon fat
$\frac{1}{4}$ pint stock (150ml)
Salt and pepper
2 tablespoons redcurrant jelly
$\frac{1}{4}$ pint red wine or cider (150ml)

Slice prepared kidneys thinly. Make a roux of the flour and butter and brown slightly. Gradually add the stock and cook for 5 minutes, stirring until thickened. Add the kidneys, season, and simmer for about 1 hour, until tender. Add the jelly, beaten slightly with a fork, the wine or cider and reheat.

Kidney stew

4 large pork kidneys
2 oz butter or fat (50g)
2 oz flour (50g)
1 pint stock (570ml)
1 dessertspoon chopped onion
Salt and pepper

Cut prepared kidneys into sections and sauté for 3 minutes in butter. Add the flour and cook for 2 minutes longer. Add the stock, onions and seasoning, cover and simmer for 1–1$\frac{1}{2}$ hours or until tender. Serve with mashed potatoes or boiled rice.

Liver

Liver in cider

1 lb calf's liver (450g)
3 tablespoons butter or margarine
1 teaspoon chopped parsley
1 tablespoon chopped chives
2 cloves
$\frac{1}{2}$ pint cider (275 ml)
Salt and paprika
2 oz sliced mushrooms (50g)
1 tablespoon flour

Slice the liver, cut into 2-inch pieces and sauté in butter for 3 minutes. Add the parsley, chives and cloves. Heat and then add the cider, and season. Add the liver and simmer (covered) for 3 minutes before removing it. Add the mushrooms to the stock and simmer (covered) for 3 minutes. Make a paste with the flour and 1 tablespoon of water (or use *beurre manié*), and add to the mushrooms, stirring well. Bring to the boil and simmer for 3 minutes, then add the liver and simmer for another 5 minutes.

Liver with mushrooms

3 oz butter or margarine (75g)
8 oz lamb's liver (225g)
4 oz sliced mushrooms (110g)
3 tablespoons white wine (45ml)
4 tablespoons sour cream (60ml)
Salt and pepper

Sauté the thinly sliced liver in the butter, turning it frequently. Add the mushrooms, wine and cream, and season. Cook until the liver and mushrooms are tender. If the sauce is too thick, thin with more wine. Serve on toast, or in a border of rice.

Stuffed liver

4 oz streaky bacon (110g)
4 tablespoons breadcrumbs
1 teaspoon lemon rind
1 teaspoon chopped parsley
2 leaves sage, chopped
1 beaten egg
1 lb sliced liver (450g)
$1\frac{3}{4}$ lb mashed potatoes (800g)
2 oz butter or margarine (50g)
Salt and pepper

Remove the rind from the bacon and chop finely. Mix with the breadcrumbs, grated lemon rind, parsley and sage. Season and bind with the egg. Place half of the sliced liver in a well-greased casserole. Top with the breadcrumb mixture and place the remainder of the liver on top. Pile the mashed potatoes over the liver, ruffle with a fork and dot with butter.

Cover the casserole and bake for 1 hour at 375° (gas mark 5). Remove the cover, increase the heat and brown the potatoes.

Ox tongue

For tenderness choose a smooth-skinned plump tongue. Soak for at least 2 hours in cold water. Put in a large stewpan with an onion stuck with cloves, a slice of carrot and bouquet garni. If the tongue is unsalted, add 1 teaspoon of salt. Add cold water to cover, bring slowly to the boil and simmer slowly until tender (2–3½ hours depending on size). Plunge the cooked tongue into cold water for a few minutes, then remove the skin. Cut away the gristle and bone from the root end.

To serve hot. Reheat the tongue in the stock and serve with parsley sauce.

To serve cold: Put the tongue in a round tin and place a plate with a heavy weight on top. When cold, glaze with a meat glaze.

Pig's puddings

Pig's pudding (black)

Sausage skin
2 pints sheep or pig's blood (1140ml)
Salt
¾ pint milk (425ml)
8 oz chopped onions (225g)
1½ lb oatmeal (675g)
Salt and pepper
1 lb chopped leaf lard (450g)

Wash the skins in salt and water, scrape them, turn them inside out and wash and scrape again. Let them soak in salted water for 24 hours, then give them several rinsings in clear cold water. Pat them as dry as possible in a tea-towel. Cut them into convenient lengths (about 1 yard), and tie one end.

While the blood is still warm, add a teaspoon of salt and stir until the blood is cold (this is to prevent coagulation). Add the milk, onions, oatmeal and seasonings, and mix well. Put in enough of the mixture to make a sizeable pudding. Tie again, leaving the pudding plenty of room to swell in the boiling. Now make another tie about 1 inch from the last and make another pudding (there should be about 3 to every length of skin). Separate them with a snip of the scissors. Prick well with a darning needle to prevent bursting while cooking, and put them into boiling water for 1 hour. When you take them out, pat them dry in a tea-towel and hang them up to dry.

Pig's pudding (white)

1½ lb oatmeal (675g)
6 oz parboiled chopped onions (175g)
12 oz chopped leaf lard (350g)
Salt and pepper

Toast the oatmeal until light brown. Mix all the ingredients thoroughly and season well. Fill the skins, and cook as for black puddings.

Note: Instead of toasting the oatmeal, some cooks like to soak it overnight in a pint of milk. To give extra flavour, add 8 oz (225g) of liver, parboiled and chopped finely.

Tripe

Your butcher will supply blanched and pre-soaked tripe. To cook, cover with stock or water, add a bouquet garni and simmer for about 30–60 minutes (the length depends on whether you like your tripe 'chewy' or softer).

Fried tripe

Cut cooked tripe into squares or strips and season. Dip in batter and fry in deep fat. Serve with tartare sauce.

Geneva tripe

1½ lb tripe (675g)
4 tablespoons breadcrumbs
3 tablespoons butter or bacon fat
12 oz sliced tomatoes (350g)
¼ pint stock or water (150ml)
Salt and pepper
2 tablespoons grated cheese

Cut the tripe into thin strips. Lightly brown the breadcrumbs in the butter, add the skinned tripe, tomatoes, and seasoning. Pour in the stock, cover and simmer for 10 minutes. Stir well cheese into the mixture and serve at once.

Tripe and onions

1½ lb tripe (675g)
1 lb sliced onions (450g)
2 pints scalded milk (1140g)
Salt and pepper
3 oz butter or margarine (75g)
3 oz flour (75g)

Cut the tripe into 3-inch strips, about 1½ inches wide. Place in a casserole with the onions and the milk, and season. Cover and cook for 2 hours at 300° (gas mark 2). Make a roux with the butter and flour, gradually add milk stock from the tripe, bring to the boil, stirring well, and simmer for 3 minutes. Pour over the tripe and serve with toast.

Tripe in gravy

2 lb tripe (900g)
1 pint water (570ml)
2 tablespoons vinegar (30ml)
1 chopped onion
4 cloves
Salt and pepper
3 oz butter (75g)
3 oz butter or margarine (75g)

Cut the tripe into small pieces. Place in a saucepan and add the water, vinegar, onion, cloves, salt and pepper. Cover and cook for 2 hours at 300° (gas mark 2). Make a roux with the butter and flour, blend with some of the stock, return to the saucepan and cook for another 5 minutes, stirring constantly.

Spanish tripe

2 lb tripe (900g)
2 oz butter (50g)
3 tablespoons chopped onion
1 clove garlic
1 small sliced carrot
2 tablespoons chopped parsley
½ bay leaf
¼ teaspoon dried thyme
2 teaspoons lemon juice
1 tablespoon flour

¾ pint boiling water (425ml)
Salt and pepper

Cut the tripe into strips. Sauté in butter, the onion, garlic and carrot. Add the tripe, parsley, bay leaf, thyme and lemon juice. Toss over a low heat for 2 minutes, then sprinkle with flour. Add the boiling water, season, cover and simmer for 20 minutes. Stir frequently (tripe burns easily).

Sweetbreads

To ensure whiteness, sweetbreads must be blanched before cooking. Put them into a basin with a teaspoon of salt, cover and leave for 1 hour. Drain, put into fresh water, bring to the boil, then strain off the water. When the sweetbreads are cold, skin and remove all fibres and pipes.

Creamed sweetbreads

1 lb calf or lamb sweetbreads (450g)
1 small sliced onion
A little mace
Salt and pepper
¾ pint stock (425ml)
1 oz butter (25g)
1 tablespoon flour
1 beaten yolk
2 tablespoons cream (30ml)

Put the sweetbreads into a stewpan, with the onion, seasoning and stock. Cover and simmer gently for 1 hour. Blend the butter and flour and cook over a low heat for 3 minutes. Strain the stock in which the sweetbreads were cooked and add to the roux, stirring all the time. Bring to the boil and cook for 5 minutes. Take the pan from the fire, pour a little of the hot mixture on to the well-beaten yolk and the cream, mixing well. Put the sweetbreads into this sauce, reheat but do not boil. Serve with slices of lemon.

Sautéed sweetbreads
Simmer 4 lamb sweetbreads in ½ pint (275ml) of milk for 10 minutes. Then sauté in butter until brown on both sides. Serve with sautéed and puréed tomatoes.

Poultry and Game

Chicken

For roasting, frying or grilling, poultry must be young, and it should be plump but not too fat. If buying fresh chickens (i.e. not oven ready), look for the distinguishing signs of youth — comb bright, soft and smooth, legs smooth, pliable cartilage at the end of the breastbone.

All roast poultry benefits from larding. This can be done in the difficult way, with larding needles and strips of fat. Or it can be done easily by covering the breast with fat bacon. To improve the colour of boiled or steamed chicken or turkey, rub with a slice of lemon before cooking.

If the chicken is a little elderly, remember that the juices and flavour which time has stolen from the bird must be restored in the cooking. It needs lengthy cooking in a well-flavoured stock or sauce.

Boiled chicken

Use just enough water to cover the chicken completely. Add ½ teaspoon of salt, a bouquet garni, bring to boiling point and reduce the heat. Simmer until the bird is cooked.

Braised and stuffed chicken

1 sliced onion
1 sliced carrot
4 diced bacon slices
1 pint stock or water (570ml)
1 4-lb fowl, stuffed
1 teaspoon mixed herbs
12 peppercorns/6 cloves
3 bay leaves
Salt and pepper

Put the onion, carrot and half of the bacon in the bottom of a heavy saucepan. Place the fowl on top, add the rest of the ingredients, and then the stock or water. Cover the fowl with some greased paper, cover and let it simmer steadily for 2 hours, basting occasionally over the paper. When it is tender, take off the paper, lift out the fowl, dredge with flour, sprinkle with melted butter and brown quickly in a hot oven.

Strain the liquid in which it was cooked and thicken with *beurre manié* to make a sauce for serving.

Chicken galantine	1 3-lb fowl 8 oz minced ham (225g) 8 oz sausage meat (225g) 1 beaten egg 1 teaspoon dried herbs ½ pint stock (275ml) 1 stock chopped celery 2 sliced carrots 2 sliced onions 6 peppercorns Sprig of parsley ¼ teaspoon gelatine

This is an excellent dish for eating with salad. Joint and bone the fowl, cut into slices, and put a layer of the meat on a well-buttered cloth. Now spread over it a layer of foremeat made by combining the ham, sausage meat, egg and herbs. Repeat these layers, finishing with a layer of chicken. Roll it up in the cloth, stitch or tie securely, and put into a casserole with the stock, celery, carrots, onions, peppercorns and parsley. Cover closely and simmer for 3 hours.

When cooked, take from the casserole, drain and let it cool. Remove the cloth and turn the galantine on to a dish. Soak the gelatine in 1 tablespoon of cold water, add to the strained stock, and cover the chicken with this glaze. Salt to taste.

Chicken with Hollandaise sauce	1 boiling fowl Stock or water 4 sprigs parsley 1 onion stuck with cloves

4 peppercorns
Salt
Boiled rice

Simmer the fowl until tender in the stock, to which has been added the parsley, onion and peppercorns. Season. When cooked, joint the fowl and remove the skin. Place the pieces of fowl (they should be kept as large as possible) on hot boiled rice and mask with Hollandaise sauce.

For special occasions, add 4 to 5 asparagus tips to each helping of fowl and rice before coating with Hollandaise.

Chicken stew with dumplings

1 boiling fowl
2½ pints stock or water (1400ml)
1 onion stuck with cloves
Salt and pepper
2 sliced carrots
1 tablespoon flour
1 tablespoon butter
1 recipe Butter Dumpling Batter
Parsley

Joint the fowl, and place in a pot with the stock. Add the onion and season. Simmer for 3–3½ hours or until it is very tender, adding the carrots 30 minutes before the fowl is cooked. Skim off the fat. Thicken the gravy with *beurre manié*. Bring to the boil, drop in the dumpling batter by tablespoons, cover and simmer for 12 minutes. Put into a hot serving dish, and sprinkle with chopped parsley and paprika.

Chicken and onion stew

1 boiling fowl
2 large finely chopped onions
Salt and pepper
½ pint stock (275ml)
1 teaspoon vinegar

Joint the fowl. Sauté the onions in butter until tender and put into a casserole with the seasoning and vinegar. Add the fowl and the stock. Cover closely and simmer until tender at 350° (gas mark 4).

Chicken stew (Brunswick)

1 4-lb boiling fowl
2 tablespoons bacon fat
3 tablespoons chopped onion
12 oz quartered tomatoes (350g)
1 pint stock (570ml)
6 cloves
Salt and cayenne pepper
2 lb halved potatoes (900g)
12 oz sliced French beans (350g)
2 teaspoons Worcester sauce
1 cup toasted breadcrumbs

Joint the fowl and sauté slowly until light brown in the fat. Remove, and then sauté the onions. Put the chicken and onions into a large stewing pan, add the tomatoes, boiling stock, and seasoning. Simmer (covered) until the chicken is nearly tender. Then add the potatoes and French beans, and continue cooking until the vegetables are tender. Remove chicken and vegetables to a serving dish. Season the gravy with salt and Worcester sauce. At the last minute, stir in the toasted breadcrumbs.

Chicken and rice casserole

1 4-lb boiling fowl
Salt and pepper
4 slices fat bacon
1 chopped onion
8 oz tomatoes (225g)
1 bay leaf
2 cups stock or water
4 oz cooked rice (110g)

Joint the fowl and season. Dice the bacon and fry for a few minutes, then sauté the onions and tomatoes in the fat. Put the fowl, bacon, onions, tomatoes and bay leaf in a large casserole. Rinse the frying-pan with the stock and pour over the fowl. Cover and cook for $1\frac{1}{2}$–2 hours at 325° (gas mark 3).

While the fowl is cooking prepare the rice. When cooked, add the rice and return to the oven for about 15 minutes.

Chicken	1 3-lb chicken
Parisienne	3 tablespoons flour
	4 tablespoons butter
	2 tablespoons brandy
	½ teaspoon chopped garlic
	1½ cups chicken stock

Cut the chicken into pieces and remove the skin. Dust lightly with flour and brown quickly in 3 tablespoons of butter. Heat the brandy, pour over the chicken and ignite. Sauté the garlic in the rest of the butter for 30 seconds, add the rest of the flour and stir until smooth. Remove from the heat, gradually add the stock, stirring constantly, and continue cooking until it begins to boil. Season and add to the chicken. Cover and simmer for 25 to 30 minutes.

Fried chicken
Joint a very young chicken. Shake in a bag containing seasoned flour, then fry for about 10 minutes in deep hot fat. Drain on paper.

Another method is to simmer the chicken in salted water until almost tender. Drain, cool and cut into pieces for serving. Roll in seasoned flour, and fry until brown in hot fat or butter, turning twice.

Grilled chicken
Choose a very young chicken or 2 *poussins* (baby chickens weighing about 1 lb). Quarter the chicken or split the poussins into two. Brush with oil or melted butter. Place on the grill, with the skin side towards the heat. Grill moderately slowly about 3 inches from the heat. The chicken will be cooked in 10 to 15 minutes, depending on size.

Curried	1 boiling fowl
chicken	Salt and pepper
	2 cups stock
	2 tablespoons butter or bacon fat
	1 chopped apple
	1 chopped onion
	3–4 chopped mushrooms

1 dessertspoon curry powder
1 dessertspoon flour
2 tablespoons cream or top of bottle
4 oz rice (110g)

Joint the fowl, season and simmer in the stock until tender. Remove and keep hot. Melt the butter in a frying pan, and add the apple, onion and mushrooms. Thicken the stock in which the fowl was cooked with *beurre manié*, add the curry powder and simmer gently until smooth and thick. Put the chicken pieces into the sauce and heat thoroughly but do not boil. Just before serving add the cream.

Prepare plain boiled rice, make a border on a large dish, and put the curried chicken in the middle.

Roast chicken
Stuff the chicken and place on a rack in a baking tin. Brush with butter and cover the breast with a couple of slices of bacon. Roast at 450° (gas mark 8), basting frequently. Ten minutes before it is cooked, remove the bacon to allow the breast to brown.

The stuffed bird should be weighed before putting it into the oven. Allow 45 minutes for a 2-lb chicken, 55 minutes for $2\frac{1}{2}$ lbs, 1 hour for 3 lbs, 1 hour and 10 minutes for $3\frac{1}{2}$ lbs.

Serve with bread sauce, boiled ham or bacon, rolled rashers, and fried sausages. Brown gravy flavoured with tarragon is the ideal sauce.

Roast chicken, casserole style
Rub all over with seasoned flour and brown quickly in butter in a heavy pan on the top of the stove. Transfer to a large heavy saucepan. Pour $\frac{1}{2}$ cup of boiling stock into the pan, cover and cook very slowly under tender. The time will depend on the age of the chicken.

Chicken can also be cooked in this way in the oven.

Steamed chicken
Put the chicken into a bowl or pan with enough water to cover it. Place the bowl in a large saucepan and add sufficient boiling water to come three-quarters way up the side of the bowl.

Cover and boil gently until the chicken is tender. A 2½-lb chicken will take about 2 hours, 15 minutes.

Or place the chicken in a steamer, cover closely and steam over gently boiling water.

Duck

Duckling Rineanna	This delicious dish was created by Chef Ryan of Shannon Airport Restaurant

4 large peeled and quartered apples
2 oz butter (50g)
½ pint cider (275m)
Salt and pepper
1 teaspoon each chopped parsley and fennel
⅛ teaspoon grated nutmeg
4 oz breadcrumbs (110g)
1 4-lb duckling
½ teaspoon chopped mint
1 dessertspoon arrowroot
4 cored apples

Cook the quartered apples in the butter over a slow heat. When cooked, add ¼ pint of cider, and cook for another 10 minutes. Season, and add the parsley, fennel and nutmeg. Mix well, and add enough breadcrumbs to absorb the liquid so as to give a moist stiff stuffing. Stuff the duck with this mixture, dredge with flour and put into a roasting tray. Cook at 450° (gas mark 8) for 40–45 minutes. Remove from the oven and keep hot. Strain off the pan liquor into a saucepan, add the rest of the cider and reduce it to half its volume, taking care to skim off all grease. Add the mint and thicken with the arrowroot dissolved in stock.

Place the duck on a serving dish and surround with the cored apples which have been cooked slowly for about 25 minutes. Cover with the sauce.

Roast duck
For roasting, duck should not be more than 3 months old. Birds of this age have pliable yellow feet and firm breast.

Place on rack in a baking pan, and cover the breast with slices of fat bacon. Roast at 450° (gas mark 8) for 50 minutes (for a 2-lb bird) and allow 10 minutes for each extra $\frac{1}{2}$ lb. Serve with orange sauce.

Goose

A goose weighing between 8 to 10 lbs, and not more than 12 months old, roasts best. Look for; pliable yellow feet, white skin, smooth yellow bill.

Singe and clean the goose, cut off the neck, wash thoroughly inside and out and dry well. Rub the inside with 1 teaspoon of salt and a cut lemon. Stuff with potato stuffing or sage and onion stuffing. Truss and prick the skin well with a sharp fork to allow the excess fat to run out. Place, breast down, on a rack in a baking tin and roast at 325° (gas mark 3) for 3–3½ hours (for an 8 to 10 lb bird), 3½–4 hours (for a 10 to 12 lb bird); these weights refer to the stuffed oven-ready bird.

When half done, turn the goose breast side up and finish roasting. Serve with apple sauce or brown gravy.

Turkey

Hen birds roast best, and the best weight is around 10 lbs. Cartilage at the end of the breastbone should be pliable, skin white, legs smooth.

Roast turkey

After washing out the turkey under a running tap, give it a second washing in cold water containing bread soda — one teaspoonful to each quart of water. Now give it a third rinsing in clear water. The bread soda will neutralize any sourness or unpleasantness which may exist if the bird has been lying undrawn for some time.

Dry the bird and rub the inside with $\frac{1}{2}$ teaspoon of salt. Stuff the body and crop lightly. Fasten the neck skin to the back of the bird with a skewer. Stitch up the body opening, or fasten by running a skewer through back and front and lacing tightly with string. Tie the drumsticks tightly to the tail. Twist the wings so that the tips come on to the back. Brush the bird with melted fat. Lay a few very fat rashers over the breast and tops of the drumsticks. Wrap the bird in aluminium foil and place on a rack in a shallow baking tin and cook according to the following time-table:

5–8 lbs	325° (gas mark 3)	$3\frac{1}{2}$–4 hours
8–12 lbs	325° (gas mark 3)	4–$4\frac{1}{2}$ hours
12–16 lbs	300° (gas mark 2)	$4\frac{1}{2}$–5 hours

When the turkey is three-quarters cooked, remove the foil and the rashers, baste with dripping and roast until brown and tender.

If preferred, the foil may be omitted and the juiciness of the breast and drumsticks preserved in this way: Lay the trussed bird breast downwards on the roasting rack. Cover with a thin cloth moistened with melted bacon fat or melted butter. Remoisten the cloth with fat from the pan if it dries out during cooking. One hour before the turkey is cooked, turn it breast side up, remove the cloth, baste with drippings from the pan and continue roasting until brown.

Serve with bread sauce, giblet gravy, and sausages.

Game

Game should be hung for at least 1 week before cooking. Hang in a cold place where the air may circulate fully around it.

Only young birds are suitable for roasting. Signs of youth are smooth legs, pliable feet, soft quill feathers in the wings.

Grouse, partridge and pheasant are drawn and trussed like chicken. As grouse is too small for drawing in the usual way, the entrails are squeezed out at the neck opening. Snipe, plover, quail and woodcock should not be drawn.

Braised game

Place the giblets in a stewpan with bouquet garni, a blade of mace and $\frac{1}{2}$ pint (275ml) of stock or water. Place the game on the giblets, and cover with slices of fat bacon. Cover and simmer until tender (this will depend on the age of the birds — young birds take about an hour). Remove the bacon 10 minutes before the birds are done. When cooked, place on a hot dish, skim the stock, strain and reduce by fast boiling to ¼ pint (150ml). Pour over game and serve with game chips and bread sauce.

Casserole of game

Prepare a brace of grouse or partridge (or 1 pheasant) as for roasting and cover with slices of fat bacon. Dice 1 stick of celery, 1 carrot and 1 onion. In a casserole, melt 1 oz (25g) of butter, and add the game and vegetables. Pour in ½ pint (275ml) of giblet stock, cover closely and cook for 2 hours at 325° (gas mark 3). Place the birds on a hot dish and keep warm.

Strain the liquor from the casserole into a saucepan, add ½ teaspoon of anchovy sauce, ½ glass of port wine and season to taste. Bring to the boil and thicken with a little *beurre manié*. Simmer for 5 minutes and pour over the birds.

Grilled game

Cut prepared birds in half and wipe with a damp cloth. Brush with oil or butter, season lightly and grill 3 inches from the heat. Allow 6 to 12 minutes for each side, according to the size of the bird.

Roast game

To roast partridge or woodcock, tie 2 rashers of fat bacon around the trussed bird. Place on a rack in a baking tin, with slices of bread underneath to catch drippings. Roast for about 35–45 minutes at 450° (gas mark 8).

Pheasant is roasted in the same way as chicken.

Serve roast game with bread sauce, giblet gravy, fried breadcrumbs (optional), watercress and game chips.

Rabbit and hare

Rabbit and hare can be boiled, stewed or roasted in the same way as chicken (the time will depend on age and size).

To whiten rabbit flesh, soak it for 30 minutes in vinegar and water before cooking (2 tablespoons of vinegar to 1 pint of water). Cooked rabbit may be used in any of the recipes for cooked chicken.

Jugged hare or rabbit	1 rabbit or hare
	2 oz flour (50g)
	Salt and pepper
	3 oz butter or dripping (75g)
	½ pint stock (275ml)
	1 glass red wine
	1 onion stuck with cloves
	½ teaspoon grated lemon rind
	1 blade mace
	Bouquet garni
	1 cup poultry stuffing

Joint the rabbit or hare, and roll the joints in seasoned flour. Brown quickly in 2 oz of butter, remove from the pan and sprinkle in the rest of the flour. When it is browned, stir in the stock and wine, and bring to the boil. Place the rabbit in a casserole, add the onion, lemon rind, mace and bouquet garni. Cover and simmer for 1–1½ hours for rabbit, 2–3 hours for hare.

Shape the stuffing into small balls and brown in butter. Place the rabbit on a serving dish, surround with the stuffing balls and pour over the strained gravy. Serve with redcurrant sauce

Smothered rabbit or hare
Joint the rabbit, roll in seasoned flour, and brown quickly in 3 tablespoons of butter. Cover with sliced onions, and a sprinkling of parsley and thyme. Add ½ pint (275ml) of stock, or a mixture of stock and cider or red wine. Cover closely and simmer until tender over a low heat or in a moderate oven.

Stuffed braised rabbit or hare	1 cup cooked rice
	4 oz chopped mushrooms (110g)
	1 chopped onion
	4 oz sausage meat (110g)
	2 eggs
	1 rabbit or hare
	1 tablespoon flour
	1 tablespoon butter or olive oil

½ **pint brown gravy (275ml)**
1 glass red wine
Salt and pepper

Combine the rice, mushrooms, sausage meat and onion, and bind with the eggs. Stuff the rabbit with the mixture (if the rabbit is too small to take all the stuffing, shape any left over into small balls). Dredge the rabbit with flour, and brown quickly in the butter or oil. Place the rabbit in a casserole, add the gravy and wine, season, cover closely and simmer for an hour. Then place the balls of forcemeat around the rabbit and simmer for another 30 minutes or until the rabbit is tender.

Venison

There is a Munster proverb which advises against *bheith ag ithe na feola fiadh agus an fheoil-fhiadh ar an gcnoc go foill* (eating your venison while the deer is still on the mountain). For many of us, the deer will remain in their mountain haunts. But just in cause a haunch of venison should one day find its way into your kitchen, this is how you should cook it.

Roast venison
Hang the venison for from 2 to 3 weeks in a cool airy place, rubbing it over each day with a dry cloth. Wash it in warm water and dry with a cloth. Smear it all over with dripping, wrap in thickly greased paper, and then envelop it in a stiff flour-and-water paste. Now wrap it again in greased paper and tie with string. Weigh the venison and place in a hot oven (450°- gas mark 7). Allow 20 minutes per lb and baste frequently. Thirty minutes before the haunch is cooked, take it from the oven, remove the paper and paste, dredge with flour and return to the oven to brown delicately. Serve with brown gravy and with redcurrant sauce made as follows: Simmer 1 glass of port wine and 1 glass of cider with a bouquet garni until reduced by half. Stir in 2 tablespoons of redcurrant jelly. Reheat and serve at once. Venison should be served on very hot plates as the fat chills quickly and is unpalatable when cold.

Accompaniments

Dumplings

Dumplings should be as light and feathery as bog cotton (sometimes their appearance, taste, and texture give rise to the suspicion that the children have dropped old tennis balls into the stew). One way to prevent this is to drop each spoonful of batter on to meat or vegetable which will serve as a raft and ensure that the dumpling will be cooked in steam. Another way is to cook them uncovered for 10 minutes, then replace the lid and continue cooking for another 10 minutes.

Plain dumplings	12 oz flour (350g) 1½ teaspoons baking powder 1 teaspoon salt 1 oz butter or margarine (25g) Milk

Sift together flour, baking powder and salt. Add the melted butter, and sufficient milk to make a soft dough. Drop by tablespoonfuls in the stew, first dipping the spoon in water so that the dumplings may drop easily.

Butter batter dumplings
To the basic dumpling mixture, add 2 well-beaten eggs and increase the butter to 2 oz (50g). Season with rosemary.

Cheese dumplings
Add 2 tablespoons of grated cheese to the basic mixture.

Vegetable dumplings
Add 1 tablespoon of grated onion and 2 tablespoons of finely chopped parsley to the basic mixture.

Potato dumplings	4 oz mashed potatoes (110g) 4 oz flour (110g) 1 teaspoon baking powder 1 teaspoon salt 2 tablespoons chopped onion 1 tablespoon grated cheese 1 oz melted butter or margarine (25g) 1 large egg.

Combine all the ingredients. Shape into balls, and drop into boiling soup or stew. Cook in the usual way.

Game chips

Peel raw potatoes and cut in very thin slices (about ⅛ inch). Soak for 5 minutes in salted water. Drain, pat dry in a cloth, sprinkle lightly with salt and leave wrapped in the cloth until ready to fry. Fry golden brown in deep fat. Serve at once.

Stuffing

Some like their stuffing light and crumbly, while others prefer it moist and 'cakey'. For the first, wet the stuffing with milk or stock, or use no liquid at all. For the second, bind the stuffing with beaten egg. As all stuffings swell in the cooking, the bird should never be packed tightly. One cup of stuffing is ample for each pound of bird.

Apple stuffing	1 lb cooking apples (450g) 2 tablespoons stock or water 2 oz breadcrumbs (50g) 1 egg 1 oz melted butter or margarine (25g) 1 oz sugar (25g)

Peel and slice the apples and simmer until almost tender in the stock. Add the remaining ingredients and mix well. Use for duck, goose or pork.

Breadcrumb stuffing de luxe

6 breakfastcups breadcrumbs
Salt and pepper
4 oz chopped ham (110g)
1 medium chopped onion
1 tablespoon grated carrot
6 sticks chopped celery
1 dessertspoon chopped parsley
$\frac{1}{2}$ teaspoon thyme
$\frac{1}{4}$ teaspoon grated nutmeg
$\frac{1}{2}$ teaspoon grated lemon rind
4 oz melted butter (110g)

Mix together all the dry ingredients. Add the melted butter slowly, mixing with a fork until lightly blended. If a moist stuffing is required, add a cup of cream or top of bottle. This quantity is sufficient for a 10-lb turkey.

Celery stuffing

2 cups breadcrumbs
1 cup fineiy chopped celery
2 tablespoons chopped onion
1 dessertspoon chopped parsley
$\frac{1}{2}$ teaspoon thyme
Salt and pepper
2 oz melted butter or margarine (50g)

Mix together all the dry ingredients. Add the melted butter, tossing with a fork until well blended.

Chestnut stuffing

3 lb chestnuts (1350g)
8 oz breadcrumbs (225g)
4 oz melted butter (110g)
4 tablespoons cream (60ml)
Salt and pepper

Shell the chestnuts, cover with boiling water and allow to stand for 5 minutes. Drain and cook in boiling salted water until tender (about 20 minutes). Drain and purée. Add the breadcrumbs, butter and cream, and season. Mix lightly. (This quantity is sufficient for a 10-lb bird).

Forcemeat balls

4 oz breadcrumbs (110g)
1 oz chopped beef suet (25g)
2 oz chopped bacon or ham (50g)
1 oz chopped onion (25g)
1½ teaspoons mixed dried herbs
1 teaspoon chopped parsley
Salt and pepper
1 beaten egg

Mix the dry ingredients and bind with the beaten egg. Form into small balls and fry until brown in hot fat.

Forcemeat balls are good with braised meat and are usually added to hare about 20 minutes before it is done.

French stuffing

5 breakfastcups breadcrumbs
4 oz chopped cooked mushrooms (110g)
6 stalks chopped celery
1 tablespoon chopped onion
1 tablespoon chopped parsley
1 teaspoon mixed herbs
Salt and pepper
1 beaten egg
¼ pint cream or milk (150ml)
4 oz melted butter or margarine (110g)

Mix together all the ingredients. This quantity is sufficient for a 10–12-lb bird, or it can be used for veal.

Game stuffing

1 pheasant's liver
2 oz fat streaky bacon (50g)
1 oz melted butter (25g)
1 cup breadcrumbs
1 beaten egg
1 dessertspoon cream
1 teaspoon each thyme and parsley
½ teaspoon majoram
¼ teaspoon powdered cloves
Salt and pepper

Chop the liver and bacon finely. Combine with the butter and pound to a paste. Add the remaining ingredients and mix well.

Parsley and thyme stuffing

1½ breakfastcups breadcrumbs
1½ oz chopped beef suet (40g)
2 oz chopped lean bacon or ham (50g)
1 dessertspoon chopped parsley
1 teaspoon thyme
Salt and pepper
1 egg or 2 tablespoons milk or stock

Combine the dry ingredients and bind with the egg, milk or stock. Excellent with veal.

Potato stuffing

8 oz streaky rashers (225g)
2 medium chopped onions
1 small head of chopped celery
2 lb cooked mashed potatoes (900g)
4 oz butter or margarine (110g)
1 cup milk
2 tablespoons chopped parsley
½ teaspoon mixed herbs
Salt and pepper

Fry the bacon until crisp, and chop. Cook the onions and celery in the bacon fat until tender but not brown. To the mashed potatoes, add the butter, milk, parsley, herbs, and season. Combine with the bacon, celery and onions and mix well.

Use with duck or goose.

Sage and onion stuffing (1)

12 oz chopped onions (350g)
4 breakfastcups breadcrumbs
1 egg
3 teaspoons dried or 6 leaves fresh sage
1 teaspoon lemon rind
¼ teaspoon dry mustard
Salt and pepper

Cook the onion in water until soft. Strain and combine with the other ingredients.

This stuffing, which is sufficient for a 10-lb goose, is improved by the addition of a finely minced goose liver.

Sage and onion stuffing (2)

2 tablespoons bacon fat
4 medium chopped onions
6 breakfastcups breadcrumbs
2 cups hot stock or water
2 beaten eggs
2 tablespoons chopped parsley
2 tablespoons chopped celery tops
2 teaspoons dried sage
2 teaspoons mixed dried herbs
Salt and pepper
4 oz sultanas (110g)

Fry the onion in the bacon fat until lightly brown. Pour the stock over the breadcrumbs, add the eggs and seasonings. Mix all the ingredients thoroughly (the use of sultanas is optional).

Sausage stuffing

8 oz sausage meat (225g)
4 tablespoons breadcrumbs
$\frac{1}{2}$ teaspoon dried mixed herbs
$\frac{1}{4}$ teaspoon grated lemon rind
$\frac{1}{4}$ teaspoon grated nutmeg
2 tablespoons stock
Salt and pepper

Mix all the ingredient thoroughly, and use for poultry or game.

Yorkshire pudding

Sift 6 oz (175g) of flour with salt. Separate 2 eggs, drop the yolks into the flour and blend. Stir in $\frac{1}{2}$ pint (275ml) of milk and beat well until frothy. Fold in the stiffly beaten egg whites.

Yorkshire pudding is usually cooked in the roasting tin under the beef, which should be on a rack. About 40 minutes before the meat is cooked, pour the batter into the hot dripping in the roasting tin. Return to the oven and cook at 450° (gas mark 8) for 30–40 minutes, or until puffy and brown. The cooked pudding should have risen at the sides and be rather flat in the centre. Pour off the fat which will have collected, cut into neat pieces and serve with the roast.

Left-overs

To make the most of left-over meat or fowl which is too scrappy for slicing and serving unadorned, serve it fried in batter, hashed or creamed, or made up into croquettes, patties and pies.

For ease of reference, this section has been subdivided into batter-coated food, croquettes, hash, loaves, meat pies and patties, miscellaneous recipes.

Batter-coated food

While this may be cooked in shallow fat, it is best cooked in deep fat. The fat should be clean and free from crumbs, etc., and heated to a temperature of 360° (gas mark 4/5), or until it will brown a cube of stale bread in 50–60 seconds.

Food to be fried in batter should first be coated generously with flour. Dip into the batter, let the excess run off, then fry from 3–4 minutes until golden-brown (do not overcrowd the saucepan). Drain on absorbent paper.

Basic recipe

6 oz flour (175g)
½ teaspoon salt
1 slightly beaten egg
1 tablespoon melted butter
⅔ pint milk (380ml)

Sift together the flour and salt. Combine the egg with the butter and milk. Stir into the dry ingredients and mix well. Let the batter stand at least an hour before cooking.

Batter with oil
Using the same basic recipe, substitute 4 tablespoons of salad oil for the butter, and reduce the milk to ½ pint (275ml)

Meat fritters
Dip small slices of cooked meat into the batter and fry quickly in deep fat.

Croquettes

Croquettes are made by combining 1 part of thick cream sauce with 2 parts of finely minced or chopped meat, fish, chicken, vegetables, etc. Mix thoroughly, season to taste, and add 1 teaspoon each of chopped parsley and onion. For extra flavour a teaspoon of mushroom ketchup may be added. Or when making the cream sauce, omit ¼ pint (150ml) of milk and substitute ¼ pint (150ml) of stock.

When the mixture is cold and stiff, form into croquette shapes, roll in seasoned flour, dip in fine breadcrumbs, then in beaten egg and again in breadcrumbs.

Though croquettes may be cooked in shallow fat, for crisp, well-shaped, non-greasy croquettes, deep fat and a frying basket are essential. The fat should *not* be smoking hot, but the temperature should be high enough to cook the outside of the croquette immediately so as to prevent grease absorption. The proper frying temperature is 360° (gas mark 4/5).

Put the croquettes carefully into the frying basket, making sure that they do not touch each other (this ensures they will brown on all sides and prevents broken burst croquettes). Lower the basket into the hot fat and cook for about 3 minutes or until golden brown. Drain on absorbent paper.

Chicken croquettes
To the basic mixture, add 2 tablespoons finely sliced mushrooms which have been sautéed in 1 tablespoon of butter. Beat in 1 tablespoon of sherry, 1 dessertspoon of lemon juice and ⅛ teaspoon of grated nutmeg.

Hash
Hash is basically a savoury mixture of mince, potatoes and/or vegetables.

Browned beef hash

12 oz minced cooked beef (350g)
2 cups grated raw potato
3 tablespoons chopped onion
Salt and pepper
¼ teaspoon celery seed
¼ teaspoon dried herbs
2 tablespoons bacon fat or butter

Combine the meat, potato and onion. Season and add the herbs. Melt the fat in a heavy frying-pan, and cook the meat mixture over a medium flame until a crust forms on the bottom. Turn and brown the other side. Stir from time to time to let the hash brown throughout. Shortly before it is done, pat it down firmly to form a cake.

Cumberland hash

1 lb cooked beef (450g)
1 tablespoon butter
3 tablespoons redcurrant jelly
2 tablespoons sherry
Salt and pepper
1½ lb mashed potatoes (675g)
1 dessertspoon parsley

Trim the fat from the meat and cut into ½-inch cubes. Melt the butter and jelly over a low heat. Add the sherry, and season. Stir in the meat, cover, and heat without boiling. Serve in a ring of hot mashed potato sprinkled with parsley.

Hash parmentier

1½ lb mashed potatoes (675g)
2 tablespoons melted butter
1 tablespoon cream (15ml)
12 oz minced cooked meat (350g)
1 dessertspoon chopped parsley
1 beaten egg
3 tablespoons grated cheese
Salt and pepper

Butter a deep round cake tin and line with a layer of well-seasoned mashed potatoes which have been beaten with a good nut of butter and a little cream. Season the cold minced meat, flavour with parsley and bind with the egg. Arrange on the layer of mashed potatoes and cover with another layer of potato. Cover the top with grated cheese and sprinkle with melted butter. Cook at 350° (gas mark 4) until thoroughly heated and browned.

Lamb hash

1 cup brown gravy
Salt and pepper
3 large parboiled potatoes
1 large chopped onion
3 tablespoons tomato purée, or
  2 chopped tomatoes
2 cups cooked lamb
2 tablespoons grated cheese
2 tablespoons breadcrumbs
1 tablespoon butter or margarine

Heat the gravy, season, and add the potatoes (sliced), onion, tomatoes and meat, which has been cut into ½-inch cubes. Pour into a casserole. Sprinkle the top with cheese and bread-crumbs. Dot with butter and bake at 350° (gas mark 4) for about 30 minutes.

Savoury mutton

1 lb minced mutton (450g)
Salt and pepper
1 tablespoon tomato sauce
1 large cooked cauliflower
½ pint cheese sauce (275ml)
2 tablespoons breadcrumbs
2 tablespoons grated cheese

Put the meat, seasoned and mixed with the tomato sauce, into a baking dish. Cut the cauliflower into pieces, place on the meat, and cover with the cheese sauce. Sprinkle with the breadcrumbs mixed with grated cheese, and bake until golden brown at 375° (gas mark 5) for about 15 minutes.

Shepherd's pie

12 oz minced cooked meat (350g)
2 tablespoons chopped onion
½ pint brown gravy (275ml)

1 lb mashed potato (450g)
1 beaten egg

Combine the meat, onion and gravy and place in a pie dish. Top with mashed potato. Ruffle with a fork and brush with the beaten egg. To prevent the meat mixture from recooking, stand the dish in a pan of hot water, and bake for 15 minutes at 400° (gas mark 6) until golden-brown.

Loaves

Beef and bacon loaf

4 slices cubed bread
½ cup warm stock or water
2 beaten eggs
8 oz minced streaky rashers (225g)
1 lb minced steak (450g)
2 tablespoons chopped onion
2 tablespoons tomato ketchup
Salt and pepper

Pour the warm stock on the bread cubes (or an equivalent amount of breadcrumbs). Add the eggs and beat well with a fork. Add the rest of the ingredients and mix well. Pack into a greased pie dish and bake for 50 minutes at 325° (gas mark 3).

Serve sprinkled with toasted breadcrumbs; or spread with a thin coating of tomato sauce and topped with browned breadcrumbs; or with a thin layer of mayonnaise sprinkled with chopped parsley and chives. It can also be glazed with aspic.

Creamed pork loaf

1 beaten egg
½ pint medium cream sauce (275ml)
8 oz chopped cooked pork (225g)
½ cup breadcrumbs
1 tablespoon chopped onion
2 tablespoons chopped parsley
Salt and pepper

Add the egg to the sauce. Mix well, then add the remaining ingredients. Placed in a greased pie dish and cook for 25 minutes at 350° (gas mark 4). Serve with brown gravy.

Turkey loaf
1 pint thick cream sauce (570ml)
1 cup turkey stock
12 oz diced cooked turkey (350g)
2 tablespoons chopped raw celery
4 tablespoons breadcrumbs
3 well-beaten eggs
Salt and pepper
12 mushrooms
1 oz butter (25g)

Add the sauce to the turkey stock, turkey, breadcrumbs, celery and eggs. Season and turn into a greased baking dish. Place the mushroom caps on top of the mixture, around the sides, and dot each with butter. Bake at 350° (gas mark 4) for about 30 minutes.

Meat pies and patties

Flaky, shortcrust or puff pastry may be used. Slits should be cut in the top crust to allow the steam to escape. Increase eye-appeal by brushing the pastry with beaten egg-and-milk before baking.

When pastry is listed in any of these recipes (unless the quantity is specified), it means 1 recipe of standard shortcrust, puff or flaky pastry from part 1 of *Full and Plenty*.

Open pies
Cut the dough into small rounds and fit these over inverted muffin or patty tins. Prick well and bake for 12 minutes at 500° (gas mark 10). When cooked, slip them carefully off the tins.

Pie shells may be made in advance and reheated when needed. They are filled with hot savoury mixtures and bound with a well-seasoned cream sauce or gravy. Served garnished according to the filling with chopped capers, parsley, grated egg white, etc.

Covered pies
Line patty tins with dough and brush the inner surface with white of egg. Fill with savoury mixture and cover with a thin top of dough, brushed on the inside with white of egg. Press

the edges together and pierce the tops. Bake for about 30 minutes at 450° (gas mark 8).

Quick patty cases
Cut the tops off small round dinner rolls and scoop out some of the inside. Dip in beaten egg-and-milk, and fry until golden brown in deep hot fat. Fill and garnish in the usual way.

Beef and celery patties	**Shortcrust pastry** **Egg white** **1 cup diced cooked corned beef** **3 tablespoons chopped cooked celery** **4 tablespoons diced cooked potatoes** **1 cup brown gravy** **1 tablespoon chopped chives** **1 tablespoon breadcrumbs** **1 tablespoon grated cheese** **Salt and pepper**

Line patty tins with thinly rolled shortcrust pastry and brush with egg white. Mix together the corned beef, celery, potatoes gravy, and chives. Fill the patty cases, top with the breadcrumbs and the cheese, and bake for 15 minutes at 425° (gas mark 7).

Beef pinwheels	**Shortcrust pastry** **1 egg white** **1 cup cooked minced meat** **1 cup grated raw carrot** **½ cup chopped onion** **½ cup well-seasoned brown gravy**

Roll the pastry to an oblong about ¼ inch thick and brush all over with egg white. Combine the meat, carrot, onion and gravy, and spread on the pastry, leaving about an inch of the dough uncovered at the edges. Roll up loosely, moisten the ends with water and seal well. Moisten the sides and seal. Bake for about 30 minutes at 450° (gas mark 8). Cut into slices to serve.

Chicken and ham patties

½ pint medium cream sauce (275ml)
1 beaten egg
Salt and pepper
1 dessertspoons sherry (10ml)
4 oz diced cooked chicken (110g)
4 oz diced cooked ham (110g)
2 tablespoons chopped cooked celery
1 tablespoon chopped parsley

Heat the sauce and add the egg, stirring over boiling water until the mixture thickens (do not allow it to boil). Season, remove from the heat and add the sherry. Combine with the chicken, ham, celery and parsley. Fill baked patty shells with the mixture, place for a few minutes in a moderate oven, and serve very hot.

Chicken vol-au-vent

12 oz puff pastry (350g)
1 beaten egg
2 oz sliced mushrooms (50g)
1 tablespoon butter
½ pint thick cream sauce (275ml)
6 oz cooked diced chicken (175g)
1 tablespoon sherry (15ml)
Salt and pepper

Roll out the pastry ½ inch thick, cut into 4 rounds and place on a greased baking sheet. With a smaller cutter, cut rounds about half way through the pastry. Brush with beaten egg and bake for 25 minutes at 475° (gas mark 9). Lift the centre rounds from the cooked pastry with a pointed knife and gently scoop out some of the inside. Sauté the mushrooms in butter, add to the sauce with the chicken and the sherry, and heat. Divide the mixture between the 4 cases, put into the oven for a few minutes and serve very hot.

Cornish pasties

4 oz butter or margarine (110g)
8 oz flour (225g)
4 oz lean raw meat (110g)
4 oz raw potato (110g)

2 oz onion chopped onion (50g)
Salt and pepper

Rub the fat into the flour and bind to a stiff dough with water. Roll out ⅛ inch thick and cut into 4 circles about 6 inches in diameter (use a side plate as a stencil). Combine the meat, potato and onion, and season. Divide the filling between the four circles of pastry, placing a mound in the centre of each. Moisten the edges with water and fold over in half. Crimp the edges securely together, and make a hole in the top to allow the steam to escape. Bake for 15 minutes at 400° (gas mark 6), then reduce the heat and continue baking for another 45 minutes.

(This is included in the left-over section, as cooked meat and vegetables can also be used — in this case, reduce the cooking time.)

Cumberland patties

1 tablespoon butter
3 tablespoons redcurrant jelly
2 tablespoons sherry (30ml)
Salt and pepper
12 oz cubed roast beef (350g)
1 dessertspoon chopped parsley

Melt the butter, add the redcurrant jelly, then the sherry. Season. Stir in the beef, heat without boiling, and fill cooked patty shells with the mixture. Sprinkle with parsley.

Ham and cheese pie

1 cup each sliced cooked carrots and potatoes
8 oz chopped cooked ham (225g)
1 tablespoon chopped parsley
1 tablespoon chopped chives
¾ pint medium cream sauce (425ml)
Cheese pastry
A little beaten egg

Grease a casserole and arrange in layers the carrots, potatoes and ham, sprinkling each layer with parsley and chives. Add the cream sauce. Moisten the edge of the casserole with water. Cover with cheese pastry, prick with a fork, brush with egg and bake for 25 minutes at 425° (gas mark 7).

Ham turnovers

8 oz minced cooked ham (225g)
2 tablespoons chopped pickles
1 tablespoon chopped onion
1½ tablespoons tomato catsup
¼ pint medium cream sauce (150ml)
Shortcrust pastry
1 beaten egg

Cover the ham, pickles (optional), onion and tomato catsup with the sauce, and mix well. Roll out the pastry ¼ inch thick and cut into squares. Place as much filling on the squares as they will hold. Moisten the edges and fold over to form triangles. Pinch to seal and brush with beaten egg. Place on a greased baking sheet and bake for 20 minutes at 450° (gas mark 8).

Miscellaneous recipes

Chicken casserole (quick)

3 cups cooked macaroni or spaghetti
2 cups diced cooked chicken
1 tin cream of mushroom soup
2 tablespoons breadcrumbs
Salt and pepper

Put the macaroni into a casserole. Add the chicken and season. Cover with the undiluted soup and top with crumbs and dot with butter. Place in a hot oven or under the grill until really hot and browned.

Chicken mousse

½ pint rich cream sauce (275ml)
2 well beaten eggs
4 oz chopped mushrooms (110g)
12 oz chopped chicken (350g)
Salt and pepper

Make a rich cream sauce and season. Remove from the heat, add the eggs, and mix in the mushrooms and chicken. Place in a well-greased bowl, tie down with greased paper and steam for 2 hours. Turn out and serve with mushroom sauce.

Chicken soufflé

½ pint thick cream sauce (275ml)
1 cup chopped cooked chicken
2 tablespoons each chopped cooked
  celery, carrots, onions
3 beaten yolks
⅛ teaspoon grated nutmeg
Salt and pepper
3 stiffly beaten egg whites

Make a thick cream sauce and add the chicken and vegetables. Bring slowly to the boil, simmer for 5 minutes, then remove from the heat. Add the egg yolks, stir and cook for another minute but do not allow to boil. Season. Allow the mixture to cool, then fold in the whites. Bake in an ungreased baking dish at 325° (gas mark 3) for 40 minutes or until the soufflé is firm. Serve at once.

Ham, devilled

6 slices boiled ham
2 tablespoons butter or margarine
1 tablespoon vinegar
¼ teaspoon dry mustard
Dash of pepper

Sauté the ham in the butter until slightly browned. Spread with the vinegar, mustard and pepper, roll up, reheat in the pan and serve with creamed potatoes and peas.

Ham and egg moulds

12 oz finely chopped cooked ham (350g)
8 oz grated cheese (225g)
6 eggs
1½ oz butter (30g)
Paprika

Mix the ham and cheese. Use two-thirds of the mixture to line 6 large greased muffin tins. Break a raw egg into each. Make a ring of the rest of the ham and cheese mixture around each egg. Place a nut of butter and a dash of paprika on each egg yolk and bake at 350° (gas mark 4) for about 20 minutes or until the eggs are firm.

Ham timbales

6 tablespoons scalded milk
2 slightly beaten eggs
1 tablespoon bacon fat
4 tablespoons breadcrumbs
8 oz minced ham (225g)
Paprika

Gradually add the milk to the eggs, then add the bacon fat, breadcrumbs and ham. Season. Mix well and turn into well-buttered custard cups or individual moulds. Place in a pan of hot water and bake at 350° (gas mark 4) for about 30 minutes or until a knife inserted in the centre comes out clean. Serve hot with tomato purée, or cold on a bed of lettuce.

Ragout of turkey or goose

1 tablespoon flour
2 tablespoons butter or margarine
¾ pint turkey stock (425ml)
Salt
⅛ teaspoon grated nutmeg
½ teaspoon Worcester sauce
12 oz cooked turkey or goose (350g)
1 tablespoon sherry (15ml)

Brown the flour in the butter, stirring constantly, then add the stock and cook until thickened. Season with salt, nutmeg and Worcester sauce. Add the diced turkey or goose, and cook for about 10 minutes until thoroughly heated. Stir in the sherry, bring almost to the boil and serve at once.

Scalloped turkey

4 oz cooked macaroni (110g)
1 cup cooked celery
2 cups diced cooked turkey
2 cups thin cream sauce
2 tablespoons breadcrumbs
2 tablespoons grated cheese

In a greased casserole, arrange in layers the macaroni, celery and turkey, finishing with a layer of macaroni. Add the cream sauce. Sprinkle with breadcrumbs and cheese, and bake for 30 minutes at 350° (gas mark 4) until the top is well browned.

Sauces

The Foleys were nearly a year married before Sheila discovered that a wife's first duty to her husband is to cook him the kind of meals he likes, and that no marriage can be really happy unless a man is satisfied with his table treatment.

They started with everything in their favour. They were young, healthy and good-looking. The public house which Dan had inherited from his uncle brought them an adequate living. And they were wildly in love.

They had been in love from the very first minute they laid eyes on each other. That was when Sheila, who had been sent down by the Department to lecture on bee-keeping, went into Dan Foley's grocery-hardware-drapery-confectionery saloon looking for a jar of stuffed olives. Dan was not able to supply the olives, but he was able to give Sheila the kind of love of which she had always dreamed. Three months later he gave her a wedding-ring.

Sheila's trouble was that she had been reared by two refined maiden aunts who believed that if you had enough cutlery, glass and lace mats on the table, nothing else mattered. Their idea of a good square meal was a triangle of toast trimmed with a dab of dressed crab and a sprig of parsley.

For the first few months of his marriage, Dan Foley was too drunk with love to know or care what he was eating. In fact, with Sheila sitting across the table from him, it is doubtful if he would have been able to tackle anything more substantial than the celery curls with cheese soufflé which she called dinner. I will go further and say that if, during that first fine careless rapture, Dan had caught Sheila's smile while he was coping with a mouthful of steak or ham, it is probable that the man would have choked. If, now and again, he felt a certain emptiness, a peculiar gnawing, he wrote it off as the debilitating effect of love.

Now, prolonged hunger can have two effects. If a man has the qualities which turn monks into saints, fast and abstinence can drive out the devil. If, like Dan Foley, he is just an ordinary, decent hardworking husband, hunger is more likely to bring out everything that's bad in him.

The young couple were barely six months married when Dan, to his horror, found himself snapping at Sheila one morning when she asked him a simple question. It happened just as she put his breakfast before him — two sardines beautifully arranged on a postage stamp of toast.

Sheila burst into tears, whereupon Dan naturally acknowledged that he was a brute and a cruel, insensitive monster. They kissed and made up, Dan swearing never again to offend.

But he did offend, again and again and again. Day by day, he grew more peevish and snappy. Not realizing that these faults were but the symptoms of semi-starvation, a hurt and bewildered Sheila became convinced that her husband did not love her. Having her share of pride, she became cold and distant.

On the Saturday night Jim Regan called into Dan's pub for a pint, the marriage was well on its way to being wrecked.

Jim had a parcel under his arm. 'I can hardly wait for tomorrow's dinner,' he said. 'I've a pig's cheek here that's as plump as any I ever saw. With plenty of green cabbage and floury spuds, it will make sweet eating.'

Dan stopped dead in the act of drawing the pint. He had just come down from a tea of petit fours and watercress sandwiches which had done nothing to fill the void left by a dinner of sweetbreads with a dessertspoon of creamed potato and a teaspoon of peas. 'Pig's cheek,' he echoed faintly. He pictured it smoking hot, the tender lean marbled with pearly fat. He pictured it cold, its firm nuttiness emphasized by the sharpness of pickled onions. He swallowed. Slowly, he handed the pint across the counter. 'It's years since I tasted pig's cheek,' he said wistfully.

Jim Regan took a long drink. 'We have one every Sunday,' he confided. 'We both like pig's cheek so much that we'd nearly need two of them, though I remember the time Mary wouldn't look at it. She had vegetarian notions when we married. Used to serve me up nut rissoles, I thank you! But I soon put a stop to that. I went home to my mother for dinner every day until I brought her to her senses. Since then, we've never had a sharp word.' He finished his pint. 'Aye, indeed,' he said. 'A woman won't ever be happy till you let her see who's boss.'

Dan Foley was never slow to act on good advice. He took a pound note from the till. 'Do me a favour, Jim.' His eyes were the eyes of a man who has seen the truth, and his voice was determined. 'Step over to Murphy's and get me the fellow of that pig's cheek.'

'You should have told me,' was what Sheila said with tender reproach. 'Didn't you know well I'd give you my heart for your dinner if I thought you fancied it?'

But Sheila did not confine her cooking to unadorned hearty dishes. She learned to combine substance with savour. And by increasing her repertoire of sauces, she was able to indulge her own taste for classy cooking while enhancing her husband's enjoyment of satisfying food.

And that is the whole point of a good sauce: To enhance and improve the food it accompanies.

Savoury sauces

Apple sauce

Peel, core and chop 8 oz (225g) of chopped apples, and simmer in 2 tablespoons (30ml) of water until pulpy. Beat smooth, adding 1 teaspoon of sugar, ½ oz (13g) of melted butter and 1 teaspoon of lemon juice. Serve with goose, pork or duck.

Anchovy butter

Cream 2 oz (50g) of butter or margarine until soft, then beat in 1 teaspoon of anchovy paste, and ½ teaspoon each of grated onion and lemon juice. Season with black pepper. This is delicious spread on any hot broiled fish like whiting, cod, etc. Or use it for canapés, or for spreading on a broiled steak.

Anchovy sauce
Blend 1 teaspoon of anchovy paste with 1 cup of cream sauce. Serve with fried mackerel.

Bearnaise sauce
See Hollandaise.

Black butter sauce
Season 2 tablespoons of vinegar (30ml) and boil quickly until reduced by half. Melt 2 oz (50g) of butter in another saucepan and simmer until golden-brown. Cool slightly and add $\frac{1}{4}$ teaspoon of dry mustard, 1 teaspoon of chopped parsley, salt and pepper. Serve with grilled chops or steak, fried fish or eggs.

Bread sauce
Simmer an onion stuck with cloves in water for 15 minutes. Strain off the water, add 1 pint (570ml) of milk and simmer (covered) for 5 minutes. Strain the milk over 2 oz (50g) of breadcrumbs, season, stir in 1 oz (25g) of butter and beat over warm water until it has melted.

This sauce may be made overnight and left in the fridge or a cool place. To reheat, place in a covered bowl or double saucepan and heat gently over boiling water (do not reheat in the oven or it will become a dry paste). A tablespoon of cream or top of bottle stirred into the sauce at the last moment gives a smooth glossy texture. Serve with roast chicken or turkey.

Butter sauce (cider)
Put 4 oz (110g) of butter or margarine in a saucepan, and add 4 tablespoons (60ml) of cider, 1 tablespoon (15ml) of lemon juice, 2 tablespoons of chopped parsley. Thicken with *beurre manié*. Heat thoroughly but do not allow to boil (this will cause the sauce to separate).

Serve with boiled or fried whiting, cod, or any white fish.

Butter sauce (lemon)
Omit the cider and substitute 4 tablespoons of stock.

Caper sauce
To ¾ pint (425ml) of thin cream sauce, add 2 tablespoons of chopped capers. Serve with boiled or steamed mutton.

Cheese sauce (1)
Add 3 tablespoons of grated cheese to medium white sauce. Stir over a low heat until the cheese is dissolved but do not allow to boil.

Cheese sauce (2)
Prepare a medium white sauce, and add 2 oz (50g) of grated cheese, 1 beaten egg yolk, 1 tablespoon of cream (15ml) and 1 oz (25g) of butter or margarine. Season and cook over boiling water until it thickens but do not allow to boil. Serve with fish or vegetables.

Cranberry sauce
Put 1 lb (450g) of well-washed cranberries in a saucepan with 1 oz (25g) of castor sugar and sufficient water to cover. Simmer until soft, then rub through a sieve and reheat. Serve with turkey.

Cream sauce
There are three consistencies of cream sauce. The basic recipe is the same in all cases, but the amounts of flour and butter vary according to the consistency of the sauce.

Thin cream sauce – for masking food such as boiled mutton, or vegetables, or for use in cream soups, etc. Use 1 oz (25g) of butter or margarine, and 1 oz of flour.

Medium cream sauce – for binding cream soups. Use 2 oz (50g) of butter or margarine and 2 oz of flour.

Thick cream sauce – as a base for croquettes, etc. Use 3 oz (75g) of butter or margarine and 3 oz of flour.

Melt the butter over a gentle heat and stir in the flour. Cook over a low heat for 3 minutes without browning, until the butter and flour form a paste. Stir in ¾ pint (425ml) of milk gradually, stirring constantly. Bring to the boil, and season to taste.

Devilled butter

Cream 4 oz (110g) of butter or margarine, and add ½ teaspoon of dry mustard, 2 tablespoons white vinegar, 2 teaspoons of Worcester sauce and 2 egg yolks. Season and beat well. This sauce transforms the more insipid fish such as whiting or cod.

Egg sauce

To ½ pint (275ml) of thin cream sauce, add 1 teaspoon of lemon juice, 1 hard-boiled egg, chopped small, and ½ oz (13g) of melted butter. Season.

Fish sauce

To ½ pint of thin cream sauce, add 1 dessertspoon each of lemon juice, chopped raw onion, chopped raw apple, chopped raw celery and chopped parsley.

French dressing

Mix ½ teaspoon of dry mustard with 1 dessertspoon of white wine vinegar or lemon juice, and season. Add 2 tablespoons (30ml) of olive oil, beating well. Add chopped garlic or (for flavour only) beat with a fork on which a clove is impaled.

Green sauce (1)

Place in a small bowl and beat well, 2 egg yolks and ¼ teaspoon of dry mustard. Season, and beat in 2 tablespoons (30ml) of white wine vinegar, then 1 cup of salad oil. When the sauce is thick and smooth, beat in 2 tablespoons (30ml) of cream and 2 tablespoons of chopped watercress. Delicious with cold fish.

Green sauce (2)

To ¾ pint (425ml) of thin cream sauce, add 4 tablespoons of sieved cooked peas or 2 tablespoons of sieved spinach. Serve hot with fish or vegetables.

Gravy (brown)

Drain off the surplus fat from roasting tin, leaving 1 tablespoon. Thicken the drippings by stirring in 1 tablespoon of flour and stir over a moderate heat until it forms a dry brown paste. Now add gradually ½ pint (275ml) of stock or water and 2 tablespoons of mushroom ketchup. Season to taste, bring the gravy to a boil and let it simmer, stirring constantly, for 3 minutes. Strain into a hot sauce-boat.

Gravy (turkey giblet)

Prepare the giblets as follows: Scald and scale the shanks, wash the liver, cut away the gall bladder carefully (if the gall bladder has already broken, the liver should be discarded), blanch and clean the heart and gizzard and soak the neck in cold salted water for 30 minutes. Cover the giblets with cold water, add a small carrot, a couple of stalks of celery, a few sprigs of parsley and a bay leaf. Simmer (covered) for 2 hours.

When the turkey is cooked, remove from the pan all but two tablespoons of the drippings. Blend with this 1½ to 2 tablespoons of flour (depending on how thick you like the gravy). Blend over a moderate heat until the flour forms a brown roux. Gradually add 1 pint of heated giblet stock. Season to taste and serve in a well-heated sauce-boat.

Hollandaise sauce (classic)

This sauce is to *haute cuisine* what a Dior ballgown is to fashion. It is one of the great sauces and is well worth the trouble. It is served with asparagus, artichokes, salmon, or any boiled fish.

Put 2 egg yolks in the top of a double boiler or a basin standing in a saucepan of hot water. Cut 6 oz (175g) of butter into small cubes and add, one by one, to the egg yolks, beating or stirring continually. The sauce should be fairly thick when all the butter is added; if not, let it cook a little longer (but very gently — otherwise it may separate). Remove from the heat, beat in ½ teaspoon of lemon juice or wine vinegar, and season with salt and pepper.

If the sauce does separate add a little boiling water and stir. If it separates badly, then you will have to add another egg yolk (when the sauce has cooled) and start again.

The addition of tarragon (fresh or dried) turns a Hollandaise sauce into Bearnaise sauce, which is the ideal sauce for grilled steak or baked fillet.

Hollandaise sauce (simple)

To ½ pint (275ml) of freshly made thin cream sauce, add 1 egg yolk and, drop by drop, 1 tablespoon of lemon juice or vinegar. Reheat but do not allow to boil.

Horseradish sauce

To ¼ pint (150ml) of thin cream sauce, add 2 tablespoons of grated drained horseradish and ¼ teaspoon of dry mustard. Serve with roast beef.

Madeira sauce

Combine ½ pint (275ml) of brown stock, with 2 tablespoons (30ml) of Madeira and 1 oz (25g) of butter and bring to the boil. Mix 1 teaspoon of arrowroot to a thin paste with cold water. Stir into the boiling stock and simmer for 5 minutes. Add 1 dessertspoon of tomato catsup, and bring again to the boil. Serve with meat, particularly ham.

Maitre d'hotel butter

Beat 1 teaspoon of chopped parsley into 1 oz (25g) of butter until smooth. Add salt, pepper and 1 teaspoon of lemon juice. Chill until required.

Cut into rounds and serve with chops or steak. For game, substitute cayenne for white pepper.

Mayonnaise

Combine 2 egg yolks with ½ teaspoon of dry mustard and salt. Add 1 tablespoon of lemon juice or wine vinegar and mix well. Now add, drop by drop, 7 tablespoons of olive oil. When the sauce thickens, the oil may be added more quickly.

A word of warning: If, before the sauce begins to thicken, the oil is added more than a drop at a time, the mayonnaise may curdle. To make absolutely sure of preventing this curdling, 1 cooked egg yolk may be substituted for one of the raw yolks. This trick ensures a non-curdled mayonnaise, but the finished result will not be so smooth and creamy.

Mayonnaise (chiffonade)

Mix 1 cup of mayonnaise with 2 tablespoons of chopped parsley and 1 tablespoon of chopped onion and grated carrot.

Mayonnaise (fluffy)

Fold 1 stiffly beaten egg white into 1 cup of mayonnaise.

Meat glaze

Meat glaze improves enormously any kind of cold meat, even scrappy left-overs. Reduce 1 pint (570ml) of meat stock by rapid boiling to ½ pint (275ml). Add 1 oz (25g) of gelatine and stir over a low heat until the gelatine has dissolved. Add a few drops of browning and pour into a jar.

When the glaze is required, stand the jar in warm water until the aspic has melted sufficiently to be brushed over the meat to be glazed. For special occasions, whip a few tablespoons of cream until thick, season, fill an icing syringe and pipe a pattern on the set glaze; a very effective decoration is a lattice done in cream, with a small diamond of cooked beetroot or a slice of stuffed olive in each square.

Mint sauce (1)

Mince mint finely to make about 4 dessertspoons, combine with ¼ pint (150ml) of white wine vinegar, and 2 dessertspoons of castor sugar, and stir until the sugar is dissolved. Make at least 2 hours before serving to give the vinegar a chance to become impregnated with mint flavour. Serve with lamb.

Mint sauce (2)

Simmer ¼ (150ml) of vinegar with ½ pint (275ml) of water and 2 heaped tablespoons of chopped fresh mint until reduced to half the original quantity. Remove from the heat and strain. Add 4 tablespoons of warm water, 2 tablespoons of lemon juice, 2 tablespoons of sugar and ½ teaspoon of salt. When cold, add another 2 tablespoons of chopped mint leaves.

Mushroom sauce

Sauté 3 tablespoons of sliced mushroom and 1 teaspoon of chopped onion in 1 oz (25g) of butter or margarines for 3 minutes. Stir in 2 oz (50g) of flour, and season. Gradually add ½ pint (275ml) of milk and cook over a low heat, stirring well, until the sauce thickens.

Mustard sauce

Combine 2 tablespoons of flour with 3 tablespoons of butter or margarine, and slowly stir in 1 teacup of fish or vegetable stock. Cook, stirring constantly, until thick. Add ½ teaspoon of dry mustard, salt and pepper, and cook for another minute. Serve with fried herring.

Onion sauce (1)
Combine 2 tablespoons of butter or margarine with a table-spoons of flour and cook until light brown. Mix ¾ cup of stock or cabbage water with ¾ cup milk and stir 1 cup of this into the flour mixture. Add 1 large onion, chopped small. Season, and cook until the onions are tender. Add the remainder of the milk and stock gradually and bring to the boil. The sauce should be thick with onions.

Onion sauce (2)
Simmer 2 medium onions in salted water until tender, drain and chop small. Add to ½ pint (275ml) of thin cream sauce. This sauce can be served with its 'oniony' texture or puréed to smoothness.

Orange sauce (1)
Remind the rind and pith from 1 orange. Slice thinly, removing the pips. Marinate for 1 hour in a cup of French dressing. Serve with roast duck.

Orange sauce (2)
Simmer ½ pint (275ml) of brown gravy, with 2 tablespoons of orange juice and 1 dessertspoon of lemon juice for 3 minutes. Season and add 1 dessertspoon of grated orange rind.

Parsley sauce
Add 2 tablespoons of finely chopped parsley to ½ pint (275ml) of well-seasoned thin cream sauce.

Raisin and cider sauce
Combine ½ pint (275ml) of brown stock with 2 tablespoons (30ml) of cider and 2 oz (50g) of raisins. Thicken with *beurre manié* and serve hot with ham.

Redcurrant sauce
To ½ pint (275ml) of brown gravy, add 2 tablespoons of red-currant jelly, 1 tablespoon of lemon juice, ½ teaspoon of castor

sugar, salt and pepper. Simmer for 2 minutes, then stir in ½ oz (13g) of melted butter. Serve with roast lamb or game.

Sour cream sauce
Chop 3 slices of bacon and fry slowly until crisp. Beat 1 egg, add a pinch of dry mustard, 1 teaspoon of sugar, salt and pepper. Add ¼ pint (150ml) of sour cream, stirring well. Add to the bacon in the pan and heat until just boiling.

Tartare sauce
Add 1 tablespoon each of chives, parsley, capers, tarragon and chevril to 1 cup of mayonnaise.

Tomato cream sauce
Slice 1 large tomato and sauté in 2 tablespoons of olive oil until lightly browned on both sides, adding at the last minute ¼ finely chopped clove of garlic. Beat into ½ pint (275ml) of medium cream sauce and serve hot with any fish.

Index